# FOR ALL
# WHO HAVE BEEN
# FORSAKEN

## S.D. GAEDE

**Broadmoor BOOKS**

Zondervan Publishing House
Grand Rapids, Michigan

To Uncle Waldo and Aunt Esther,
who confounded the wisdom of darkness
and pronounced my forsakenness a lie

For All Who Have Been Forsaken
Copyright © 1989 by S. D. Gaede

Broadmoor Books are published by the Zondervan Publishing House
1415 Lake Drive, S.E., Grand Rapids, Michigan 49506

**Library of Congress Cataloging-in-Publication Data**

Gaede, S. D.
    For all who have been forsaken / by S. D. Gaede.
        p. cm.
    ISBN 0-310-21130-1
    1. Consolation. 2. Rejection (Psychology)—Religious aspects—
Christianity. I. Title.
    BV4905.2.G28        1989                         88–13809
    248.8'6—dc19                                          CIP

*Edited by Linda Vanderzalm, John Sloan*
*Designed by Louise Bauer*

*Printed in the United States of America*

89  90  91  92  93  94 / AF / 10  9  8  7  6  5  4  3  2  1

# Contents

IIIIIIIIIIIIIIIIIIIIIIIIIIIIIIIIIIIIIIIIIIIIIIIIIIIIIIIIIIIIIIIIIIIIIIIIIIIIIIIIIIIIIIIIIIIIIIIIIII

You will grieve, but your grief will turn to joy. A woman giving birth to a child has pain because her time has come; but when her baby is born she forgets the anguish because of her joy that a child is born into the world. So with you: Now is your time of grief, but I will see you again and you will rejoice, and no one will take away your joy.

John 16:20–22

# 1

## Forsakenness Redeemed

||||||||||||||||||||||||||||||||||||||||||||||||||||||||||||||||||||||||||||||||||||||||||||||||||||||||||||||||||||||||||

*The deepest need of man, then, is the need to overcome his separateness, to leave the prison of his aloneness.*

Erich Fromm, *The Art of Loving*

July was easing into August. Purgatory as a college sophomore was over. I had spent the first two months of summer sweating on the family farm, earning enough fodder to carry me through another year of indulgence. I was ready for a break. Fortunately, my parents felt the same way. So the family forsook the hot, desert climate of the San Joaquin Valley in favor of the cool breezes of the California coast. Such summer treks to the beach had become a family tradition over the years, and I enjoyed them immensely. Dad would finally forget about the farm. Mom would finally forget about the kids. And the kids would take full advantage of their forgetfulness. For me, it was also a time to elude academic schedules and domestic routines. And, I must confess, I was fond of escapes.

This particular summer vacation, however, my escape was short-lived. After supper one night, as the ocean leisurely consumed a bloated, orange sun, I asked my sixteen-year-old cousin Paul to go for a drive with me. We headed down Coastal Route 1 toward Morro Bay. As we drove over a hill where some road construction was in process, we collided head-on with another car. No one knows why the accident took place. Neither I nor the passengers of the other car clearly recall the sequence of events. It could be that the other driver, confused by the construction work, was on the wrong side of the road. It's possible, as well, that I was at fault. God only knows.

The results of the accident, however, I recall vividly. My car—a '65 Pontiac GTO, with a deep metallic paint job, mag wheels, raised body, glass packs, a "389," and a four-speed—was totaled. And my body bore a striking resemblance to it. With ankle crushed, leg broken, jaw shattered, and extensive lacerations, I was in surgery most of the night and in critical condition for some time afterward. Passengers in the other car also were seriously injured, with broken bones and pains of various description.

Far, far more important than any of this, however, was the simple, painful, powerful fact that my passenger—my cousin Paul—was dead.

**A Forsaken Experience**

"Just stay still, Stan. Everything's going to be all right." The words were reassuring, but my predicament was not. I was lying in a hospital bed, left leg suspended in traction and my head suspended from all previously known reality.

*What's happened?* I asked myself over and over again. Only after hours of confused recollection was I able to gain even a hint of an answer.

At first, no one told me about Paul. Slowly, however, I began piecing together the events surrounding the accident, asking questions about his condition. Initially I was told, "Everything is fine; don't worry about a thing." In my stupor, this response was satisfactory, conforming as it did to my hopes. Eventually, however, my pastor—a close personal friend of the family—gently broke the news. His voice was warm and comforting. But the message cut through the social pretense and exploded in my ears. Paul was dead.

I had never felt anything like the pain of that moment. I had no other experience to compare it with. All I could comprehend was that my passenger, my cousin—for whom I was, by definition, responsible—was dead. Yet, I was alive.

Grief and guilt welled up together in an alliance of terror. My mind was drugged. My body was numbed by the routine of pain. But neither could protect my heart from this unspeakable horror.

As sorrow descended, unanswerable questions bubbled up to the surface. How could this have happened? Why did it happen? How could a loving, sovereign God allow such a thing to happen? To Paul? To his loved ones? To me? Especially to me. How could a moment such as this be mine? I was the vortex in a swirl of dark imponderables. And I saw no escape.

Then, out of the darkness came an answer so powerful it could not be ignored, so reasonable it could not be denied. *I was alone.* Loving parents were at my side, but I was alone. I nodded back to them in silent exchange, but I was alone. Another patient occupied the bed beside me. The hospital was pulsing with white-robed activity. The outside world hurried about its business. But it mattered not a whit. I was alone.

Loneliness of that kind isn't easy to describe. I felt a

deep sense of estrangement. Forsakenness. I felt as if the world and my place in it was out of whack. Life went on, but it seemed purposeless, meaningless, unreal. Life, in fact, was something of a farce. It played the most heartless of games, one moment setting me up with the best of times, and the next mocking my every effort to find self-respect.

It wasn't simply that I felt distant from others; I was alienated from myself. I peered into the mirror of self-reflection, and I didn't recognize my image. I was no longer the person I thought I was. That person died, with Paul, and I did not know the one who took his place.

## Forsakenness Redeemed

I don't know how long my alienation lasted. For those in the outside world who were on vacation or talking with an old friend or reading a good book, it was no doubt only a short moment. To me, however, it seemed like an eternity. I do remember how it ended, however.

I was lying there—leg in traction and head swollen beyond recognition—when my father told me that Paul's parents wanted to see me. My dazed mind snapped to attention. Why? The question threw my emotions into overdrive and to my forsakenness now were added feelings of fear and embarrassment. Though my mind raced, my mouth was wired shut and was disarmed by a swollen tongue. I could say nothing. I could only watch as my aunt and uncle came into the hospital room, walked toward my bed, and smiled.

They were smiling! It seemed inconceivable. How could they now be smiling? What could they be thinking? They had lost their son. *I* had lost their son. Had we all lost our minds?

The mystery did not stop there, however, it had only just begun. Soon it flowered into movements, expressions, and words. Grabbing my hand and holding it, they broke into my world. Understanding my predicament, they whispered in my ear, "You're our son now, too, you know." Those are words I will never forget. Nor should I. For they were not words I deserved nor expected. They were, of course, words of grace. They did not have to be spoken. The speakers were not required to do anything at all. My aunt and uncle could have simply slipped out of the situation and attempted to rebuild their lives without me. They would have been justified in so doing. Indeed, justice might even require a dash of bitterness and indignation. Their son bore no responsibility, after all. He bore only the cost. And yet, the words I heard were not the product of justice, but unmerited favor.

That was not my first experience with grace, by the way. I remember a time in grammar school when I did some unspeakable thing for which I knew a spanking was in order. My teacher knew it, too. Looking sternly in my direction, he ordered me into the coatroom (the place he kept the paddle and delivered, in no uncertain terms, a mighty justice). When he entered the coatroom, I had already assumed the proper position, hands grabbing ankles, ready to receive my just desserts. He took the paddle from its holster, stationed himself directly behind me, and with all the power his right arm could muster, delivered a swift blow—not to my derriere—but to a nearby stack of books. I looked up in surprise, only to see the smiling face of my teacher. "Don't say a word about this to your friends," he said, as he strolled out of the coatroom. Grace and gratitude. At that moment, I knew both.

But the grace I received from my aunt and uncle that day in the hospital was infintely superior to the grace dispensed by my teacher. For it was not grounded on a whim nor was it delivered without cost. More importantly, it contained an element unknown to many and exceedingly rare in the modern world. Paul's parents were not only willing to forgive. They were willing, in the midst of their loss, to reach out and include me in their world. They saw me not as one who merely needed grace, but love. Through their pain, they understood my own. In their anguish, they recognized my need. And so, from the highest reaches of heaven, they produced a reality that confounded the wisdom of darkness, and pronounced my forsakenness a lie.

And I was changed. Forever.

## Another Forsakenness

But I am not you. My story of forsakenness may be nothing like your own. I was rescued by an exceptional act of grace, after all, from two very exceptional people. But what about those who do not have aunts and uncles to pluck them from the jaws of abandonment? What about those who have been lost in a sea of rejection for years, without the slightest hint of a coming rescue? Is my experience at all relevant for them? More importantly, is my story at all pertinent to you?

Well, obviously, I don't know you. But I believe I have seen you, not only in myself, but also in the lives of others. I have seen you in a youth rejected by his peers because he is different, now wondering if there is any reason to go on living. I have seen you in a righteous old man devastated by the loss of his family and his fortune, now wondering if God has forsaken him as well. I have seen you in a young adult whose sense of security and identity were undermined by the death of a parent. I have seen you in a pastor who has gained a great reputation but somehow lost his God. I have seen you in a responsible mother whose child suddenly decides to act irresponsibly. And, I have seen you in myself as I continue to struggle daily with the effects of rejection and loss.

I have seen someone else as well, however.

His name is Jesus. And though his story is well known, evidence abounds that he is hardly known at all. As you may have heard, Jesus was a carpenter by trade but a teacher by inclination. In truth, however, he was not simply a teacher, however, since his words were matched with deeds, and his teaching always required a response.

From the beginning, he was controversial, continually doing the unexpected. He healed the sick, for one thing, and that came as quite a surprise to many. But he also confounded social conventions, talking to prostitutes one day, and outwitting lawyers the next; breaking sabbatarian rules on the one hand, but affirming the law on the other; turning water into wine on one occasion, but warning against drunkenness and sloth on the others. Tame or predictable he was not.

Well, as one might suspect, all this controversy got Jesus into a good deal of trouble. The political leaders didn't like him because he was a troublemaker and potential rival (though he claimed not to be). The

religious leaders feared his authority and were put off by
his blunt criticisms and august claims; they declared his
teachings heretical. And the common folk, though
impressed for a while, were eventually disappointed in
his style and lack of ambition. In the end, all of these
groups coalesced into one, and concluded that this man
had to go. They brought him to trial, convicted him of
treason, and sentenced him to death.

It would seem, then, that his life came to a horrible
end. Not only did he die at an early age but he died the
death of a common criminal, pinned to strips of lumber,
and disgraced through public execution. Those who had
great hopes for him were understandably disappointed:
His mother, who had watched her gifted son blossom to
maturity, wondering all the while what great things were
in store for him, now agonized as his life withered away
before her eyes. His followers, who had staked their
futures on this man, now found their future staked to a
cross, their lives thrown into chaos, confusion, and
despair. And this man who had confidently walked and
talked and lived as a man without fear or self doubt, now
cried out in gut-wrenching agony, "My God, my God,
why hast thou forsaken me?"

**Another Redemption**

At the time, those words were not well understood.
Our Source tells us that some thought he was crying out
for Elijah; they even waited around to see if Elijah would
show up to retrieve him. Others, no doubt, probably
sympathized with this man's condition, feeling that he
(and they?) had been let down by God. Even today, some
would argue that the man was finally coming to grips

with his own mortality—and surprised that God was not coming to the rescue in his moment of greatest need. To comprehend these words, however, more is needed than mere sympathy or post hoc psychology. For the same Source that records these words of despair also unfolds the story of a man whose life was like no other. At his birth, we are told, sins were forgiven. At his beckoning even the dead came to life. His birth was predicted by ancient prophets and, indeed, his coming was planned before the foundations of the earth were laid. He was, says our Source, the Messiah, the Son of God. He was with God in the beginning because he was God from the beginning. Our man, our tragic figure, was the Christ.

But God is not supposed to die. He is the Author of life, not its victim, and his Being has no beginning and no end. How can Life itself die? How can the "I AM" be no more? How can Forever cease to exist?

There are no good answers to such questions. They can be asked but they cannot be answered. By them and by the cross, we are left speechless. Stupified. And yet, strangely enough, it is only in the midst of such bewilderment that we are finally in a position to comprehend the real tragedy of Golgotha. You see, this was not simply a man falsely accused and cut down in the prime of his life, disappointing others as well as himself. This was a Man who was cut down by those he created, despised by those who should have worshiped him, mocked by those who should have trembled at his feet. But that is only the beginning. For this was a Man who was killed by those he came to save. Indeed, precisely at the moment he was being murdered by his own creation, he was, in fact, accomplishing our salvation.

This is no simple irony. It is heartrending, to be sure, but it is more than that. Jesus, at the hour of his death, was bearing the sins of the world. Not just dying, undeservedly, but dying with the weight of human sin on his shoulders. But God is holy. Righteous. Without sin. He cannot even gaze upon evil, much less enmesh himself in it. And so, mystery of mysteries, at the moment he was accomplishing our salvation, he was tearing himself in two. The holy Father was separating himself from the Son, letting the Evil One accomplish his pyrrhic victory so that you and I might be saved.

And, oh God, how it must have hurt. More than nails. More than disgrace. More than rejection. When the Father turned his back on the Son . . . what was that like, anyway? How did it feel? Words have not been conjured up for such an occasion. Nor has human experience given us feelings of comparable degree. Encased in our finitude, all we mortals have been allowed—far more than we deserve, no doubt—is to witness a moment of Trinitarian *angst;* one unfathomable question of God, by God, "Eloi, Eloi, lama sabachthani?"

**Another Possibility**

That was, of course, not only the pivotal moment in human history, but it was also the single most extraordinary experience of forsakenness ever to visit this terrestrial ball. Worse than mine, by a long shot. But even worse than yours, unless I miss my guess. And yet just think of what ensued from Christ's anguish on the cross: Nothing less than the most wonderful gift ever imparted to a sinful people. Redemption. Forgiveness. Reconciliation with God. The possibility of being what we should have been in the first place. The possibility of living forever with the One we should never have left.

It was in ruminating on the redemptive elements in Christ's forsakenness, and on my own after Paul's death, that I began wondering if we have missed ssomething in our understanding of the Cross. Understandably, we have focused on the victory of Christ over death. The resurrection, the victory of Christ over sin, is the reason for our victory as well. We lift our voices in praise on Easter for a good reason. But have we, along the way, forgotten what was required in order to accomplish that victory? Have we forgotten the words of the forsaken Christ?

I say that not to evoke feelings of pity, but exactly the opposite. The forsaken Christ forces us to realize that it was only through such cosmic alienation that we could have received such a salvation. The shocker, the wonder, the incredible thing is that the joy of redemption was predicated upon the incalculable horror of God estranged from God. We get from the Fall to Redemption in only one way—by way of the forsaken Christ.

Is there a paradigm here? Is Christ even here showing us a pattern? Could it be that hidden within every experience of forsakenness is the possibility of redemption? The possibility of learning? The possibility of new growth? Even the possibility of joy?

I think so. And this book is based on just such a possibility.

## Conclusion

We live in strange times. On the one hand are Christians who promise a life without pain or poverty;

they preach a gospel of health, wealth, and perpetual bliss. On the other hand are Christians who feel rejected, lonely, and in the depths of despair. We have them both: rose-garden Christians and forsaken Christians. Both may be genuine, but both are wrong.

The health-and-wealth gospel is wrong for a very simple reason: It's not true. The message is profoundly heretical and deeply anti-Christian, regardless of the sincerity of its promoters. We don't doubt that God rewards the faithfulness of his people. But that he always rewards by providing a life of ease and plenty is inconsistent with Scripture and patently wrong.

At the opposite end of the spectrum are those Christians who feel rejected and abandoned. Their feeling too is genuine—and even reasonable in our society—but the feeling is rooted in a lie. Nothing could be clearer in all of Scripture than the powerful, pregnant fact that God loves us. In terms of ultimate reality, we have not been forsaken. The Cross bears witness to just how much God really does love us and how much he was willing to endure to be reconciled to his creation.

Nevertheless, forsakenness still exists—not by God's preference, but through sin. And the single most obvious consequence of sin is separation. Read again the story of Adam and Eve. What happens when sin invades human existence? Humans hide from their Creator. A husband and wife quarrel. The earth frustrates its caretakers. And on it goes, continuing to this day. Sin divides. It tears us apart. In its wake, it leaves not only poverty and strife, but also forsaken people—rejected by others, estranged from themselves, and looking up and wondering, "What in the world happened to God?"

This book is about such people. In other words, it is

about you and me. It explores the personal odyssey of several people who in facing forsakenness and pain found truth and hope. In facing their despair, they found meaning. In facing their questions, they found answers and new insight. The first few chapters focus on dynamics of forsakenness familiar to many of us—rejection, feeling abandoned by God, grief, and loss. Later chapters examine several social factors that lead modern people to feel forsaken. And the final parable helps us ask ourselves how we will handle the forsakenness we experience in our own lives.

In the end, this book is an attempt to understand experiences of forsakenness, not merely for the sake of intellectual curiosity, but for the sake of Christ—who was not left to wallow in his forsakenness but through it accomplished the wonder of our salvation.

Without a doubt, Christ's forsakenness was the turning point in the story of humanity. And for that reason, our experiences of forsakenness are turning points as well. Indeed, because of Christ, every encounter with forsakenness is at once an opportunity for redemption.

# REDEEMING THE EXPERIENCE OF REJECTION

To be forsaken, literally, is to be abandoned. And we can feel abandoned for many reasons. The most obvious way we feel forsaken is when somebody rejects us. Rejection is a choice. Someone deliberately chooses to leave us out, to push us aside, to leave us alone, to forsake us.

The next two chapters will discuss two types of rejection. The first involves rejection by other people. This chapter will look at what it feels like to be rejected because of a social stigma. The second type of rejection is rejection by God. This chapter will examine the problem of pain and how it tries to separate us from God.

Both chapters will attempt to understand not only the reasons for the experiences of forsakenness but also the possible ways these experiences can be redeemed.

# 2

## *Stigma: Rejection by Others*

||||||||||||||||||||||||||||||||||||||||||||||||||||||||||||||||||||||||||||||||||||||||||||||||||||||||||||||||||||

> *It is infinitely easier to suffer with others
> than to suffer alone.
> It is infinitely easier to suffer as public heroes
> than to suffer apart and in ignominy.*
>
> Dietrich Bonhoeffer, *Letters and Papers from Prison*

I'm not always moved by modern movies. But *The Elephant Man* was an exception. Its message uncorked my emotional reservoir, flooding me with compassion, shame, and resolve. As I watched the elephant man suffer ridicule and abuse because of an external deformity, I deeply sympathized with him. His pain quickly became my own. I felt his forsakenness.

But I could identify with more than the elephant man's suffering. I also identified with the people who mocked him. I remembered all too clearly when I mimicked the spastic's walk or mumbled the moron's expressions.

In the end, however, it was the elephant man himself who rescued me from shame and lifted my spirit with resolve. If he could rise above his horrible circumstances without bitterness or envy, then surely I could rise above my insecurities and relate to others as God intended.

Would that it were so.

## Thinking About Stigmas

The elephant man's forsakenness was a result of a stigma. Because of his highly unusual physical appearance, people treated him in unusual ways. They treated him as if he were abnormal, less than human, and undeserving of respect. His peculiar physiology became his mark of distinction. It was a mark that resulted not in community concern but in social disgrace.

A standard dictionary definition suggests that a stigma is something that detracts from or defames a person's character. The word originates from a Greek word that literally means "to prick with a pointed instrument."[1] This probably refers to the once-common practice of branding or marking hardened criminals. The external mark linked the offender with the offense—forever. When sociologists use the term *stigma* today, interestingly, their thinking is more in line with the original. They consider a stigma to be a label placed upon a person by others in society.[2] Like the canner who writes "Red Raspberry" on a fresh jar of preserves, we place a label of social disgrace on those we deem inferior.

To some extent, all of us have felt the sting of a stigma. One doesn't have to be an elephant man to be stigmatized. Most of us, for example, have done something we've found difficult to live down. I remember a friend in high school, for example, who was caught cheating on an exam; though he didn't cheat often, for some time afterward, he was thought of as a "cheater." Sometimes parents will stigmatize their children, labeling one child "slow" or "crybaby" or "uncoordinated." More often than not, however, parents desperately try to remove the labels placed on their children by others. I have a large nose, for example. To counter those who would make fun of it while I was growing up, my parents periodically informed me that I had an "aristocratic nose." I wasn't sure what that meant, but I quickly became a believer. It sounded far better than the adjectives my friends used!

At times, we can even be stigmatized for traits that are considered desirable. In our society, we tend to worship intelligence and beauty.[3] Most of us try to cultivate these traits, spending gigantic sums on cosmetics and education. Nevertheless, people who are beautiful or intelligent also can become the victims of stigma. I recall a girl in junior high, for example, who developed large breasts much earlier than any of her friends. By societal standards, she had a fantastic figure. Yet, almost a decade later, she recalls those years with bitterness and tears. Why? Because her girlfriends treated her with envy, and her boyfriends considered her little more than an object. She became a one-dimensional person. Her stigma was not a social disgrace, but it was as profound in its consequences as any scarlet letter.[4]

Stigmas can also result from our identity with a particular group. Growing up in a conservative church, I wasn't supposed to go to movies or dances. I felt like a social outcast when I couldn't attend the local movie theater. Though some Christians might have worn that pain as a badge of honor, for me, it was a mark of humiliation—a stigma I wished to be rid of.[5]

My humiliation was a minor one. For one thing, I didn't have to deal with the issue on a daily basis. More importantly, however, as I matured, going to the theater became a matter of choice for me. Like most decisions of a moral nature, I was free to choose what behavior I thought was appropriate. Even if I was ostracized for my choice, therefore, I knew it resulted from my own decision.

Sometimes, however, a stigma stems not from our own choices but from the decisions of others. The elephant man is a good example. He was born with a certain physical condition, and others chose to respond in horror. He did nothing to earn their wrath. The untouchables of India, the leper of the New Testament, the black in American history, the impoverished of Appalachia—these, and many more, carry the same burden. No one chooses to be born an outcast. No one chooses a horrible disease. No one chooses to be enslaved by another race. No one chooses poverty. For these people, a stigma is hardest to bear. They can't understand it, and in most cases, they can do nothing about it. They only know that they came into a world that rejected them. They were forsaken merely for being.

### The Consequences of Stigmas

Almost inevitably, then, stigmas result in exclusion. As we said earlier, all of us are excluded from certain kinds of experiences by virtue of who we are and of our choices. But to be stigmatized is to be cut off from typical patterns of social involvement. To bear a stigma is to be excluded from normal life. That is why the consequences of a stigma are especially painful. And that is why those bearing a stigma can feel especially forsaken.

A black friend of mine described such a feeling when relating his experience at a predominantly white prep school. He had grown up in a black community, attended an urban black church, and received his education at racially mixed schools. His first lengthy experience in an all-white world, therefore, occurred when he went to a private high school. It came as something of a shock. He certainly had been exposed to white society before: he saw it on television, learned of it in school, and knew it with his heart. Like most people of color in our society, he was aware of those without color.[6] He knew, therefore, that going to a mostly white school would be socially awkward at times. What he wasn't prepared for, however, was rejection.

Few people treated him badly at the school. No one called him "nigger" or asked him to leave. But few seemed capable of treating him normally either. Two responses were typical. Some people bent over backward to show how unprejudiced they were, posturing as if interested, laughing when nothing was funny, and asking silly questions ("How do black people feel about Abraham Lincoln?"). He appreciated their intentions, of course, knowing they were just trying to be friendly. But their unusual behavior simply called attention to his stigma. It read like a flashing neon sign: "You're different . . . you're different . . . you're different."

Most people, however, just ignored him. They would pass him in the dorm or eat with him in the cafeteria or sit beside him in class and never utter a word. They acted as if he didn't exist. He began to wonder why people treated him this way. Maybe they were uncomfortable around blacks and didn't know what to say. On the other hand, he couldn't help having other suspicions. Maybe they hated blacks, he thought. Maybe, being well-trained preppies, they kept their prejudices hidden, but deep down inside they hated him. He didn't know. It had never happened to him before. And the effect was catastrophic. He was a stranger, a persona non grata. He was alone. Rejected. Forsaken.

He wanted desperately to leave—to pick up his belongings and head back to the place where he belonged. Only his pride and the high expectations of his parents kept him in school that first year. But in the meantime, he went through a personal hell. First, he doubted himself, assuming that people rejected him because of some character flaw they saw in him. Then he doubted his classmates, believing that they were all conspiring against him. After that, he became angry at the school that had recruited him, the society that labeled him, and the God who had created him. In the end, however, he lumped all his anger together and internalized it, coming back to the place he had begun, doubting his own self-worth and value. He felt, in short, like a nobody.[7]

People who bear stigmas not only are treated differently, but they also often are ill-treated. Theirs is the problem not only of not feeling like "one of the gang"— it is not being *wanted* by the gang. It is, in other words, the experience of rejection.

When stigmatized people look at themselves through the eyes of others, they feel worthless.[8] When they take the role of the other and look back at themselves, they are repulsed.[9] At that moment, they not only understand why others have excluded them, but they want to repudiate themselves as well. And self-rejection is a hard forsakenness to bear.

### Why Do We Stigmatize People?

If stigmas are such evil things, then why do we stigmatize others? After all, we don't have to stigmatize people. No one forces us to put labels on others or treat them as one-dimensional people. So why do we?

Good question. Its answer, moreover, would be so much easier if it were entirely a matter of evil intentions. If a stigma resulted simply from malevolent motives, we could identify the villains and do our best to rout them out. But it's not that simple. Sometimes a stigma is partially grounded in the desire to protect against evil behavior. How could that be?

Think for a moment about the origin of the term *stigma*. People, animals, or things were given a mark, a brand, or a label. Why would this be done? For the same reason it's done today—in order to identify them. A doctor writes "X's urine specimen" on a bottle so as not to confuse it with Y's urine specimen. A rancher puts his brand on his cows to distinguish them from other people's cows. A jailer puts a mark on a criminal in order to set him or her apart from the law-abiding citizen.

Now, all of these stigmas are understandable to the modern reader except the last. Why would the jailer need to mark a criminal? The reasons are many, but it was ostensibly done for the protection of the community. If a criminal escaped, the stigma made him or her easier to find. If a criminal was released, it put others on notice that this person was not to be trusted. If someone else was contemplating the same crime, it warned the person about the consequences of such an act. In any case, the stigma—the mark—was designed to deter future crimes, either by this or some would-be criminal. The stigma was assumed to be a way to protect the harmless from the harmful.

Let's take a more modern example. Parents sometimes say to their children things like: "Jimmy, don't play with

Suzie; she's a bad girl." In doing this, the parents place a label or stigma on Suzie. Why? They want to protect Jimmy from a harmful experience. Every time he plays with Suzie, he comes home with a bloody nose or a new four-letter word. His parents don't like it, so they do whatever they can to encourage Jimmy to play with someone else.

Notice something else. The stigma that Suzie receives, in this case, doesn't result simply from the parents' limited vocabulary. If Jimmy's parents subscribed to the *New Yorker*, for example, they might say something like: "Jimmy, given Suzie's relative mass, volitility, and propensity to fits of rage, it would be an altogether regrettable thing for you to continue playing with her." Still, Jimmy—along with his parents—knows what that means: Suzie is bonkers, and it's risky business to continue playing with her. A complex vocabulary may do much to assuage the guilt of a liberal parent, but it will do little to reduce the effects of the stigma.[10]

In each of these examples, we see that a stigma is meted out to protect others. It may not be the best way of going about this. It may needlessly hurt a lot of people along the way. It may, indeed, be just a lie. But it can at least be justified as something that achieves a greater good.

Some forms of stigmatizing, however, don't seem to fit into this pattern. Stigmatizing a criminal may be understandable from the perspective of "protecting the innocent," but why do we stigmatize someone who is merely Irish or paralyzed or from the South? Who are we protecting when we aim stigmas toward them?

To answer that question, think about your own biases and prejudices. What kinds of people really anger you?

What kinds of people do you dislike even before you meet them? Since you may be hesitant to answer such a potentially incriminating question, let me tell you about a prejudice of my own. I don't like people who make stupid comments. Nothing bothers me more than people who make silly statements, without regard for the implications or effect of those statements. When I hear such comments, I immediately make a mental note of who was talking and of how stupid the comment was. If I have future encounters with that person and if the stupid statements persist, I mark that person as a "dolt," a "social numbskull." And I want nothing further to do with them.

Now, why would I want to stigmatize another human being in this way? Well, if you asked me when others were listening, I would offer the following rationale: "Our God is the God of truth, not error. When we make comments that are not well thought through, we are acting on behalf of the Enemy. Silly comments hurt people and spread ignorance. A Christian should have nothing to do with them." My listeners would then, of course, applaud my diligent effort to expose error and fight for truth.

There is one problem with my response, however. It didn't answer the question. Everything I said was true, but it didn't explain why I put stupidity labels on others. What it did accomplish was to divert the audience from the issue of prejudicial attitudes to the topic of inappropriate behavior. It enabled me to discuss the effects of "stupid comments" rather than "stupid labels."

## Lessons for People Who Stigmatize Others

Here then is one of our first lessons about stigmas. *Stigmas usually mask as an attack on behavior, not people.* We believe stigmatizing is justified because it's part of an effort to rid the world of improper conduct. We hate the Irish because they drink too much. We can't stand Southerners because they butcher the King's English. We don't like people in wheel chairs because they act pushy and demanding. And on it goes. In every case, we identify a behavior pattern we find distasteful, associate it with a certain kind of person, and then label the person with the behavior.[11] The stigma is perceived, superficially, as a method of dealing with impropriety. In foisting the stigma on others, therefore, we think we are doing a good thing. And thus, stigmas live and breed in an atmosphere of "good people."

Those who stigmatize others, therefore, put down people for the way they act. I label someone as "stupid" because that person made a stupid comment. The label seems justified because I feel that what the person did was wrong. What escapes my attention is that this same person is *much more* than a disseminator of silly statements. He or she is a human being, much like me, with all kinds of talents, rough edges, and defects. He or she is a complicated creation of God Almighty—not a "stupid person," but someone of great value and worth.

We know that, of course. Upon reflection, most of us will admit that any stigma is a patently unfair caricature. And yet we continue to stigmatize. Why? For one thing, a stigma is the result of a complicated mix of motives, as we've seen. And complexity provides a ready smokescreen for selfish behavior. More basically, however, stigma results from sin. And therein lies the reason for its complexity. Whatever sin may be, it is not simple. Let me address the question, therefore, not with an easy answer, but with a final bit of self-reflection on stupidity labels. When I think about my reaction to "stupid people," I am struck by this discovery: There's nothing in all the world that I would rather not be called than a "stupid person." Call me ugly, and I'll shrug my shoulders. Tell me I'm boring, and I'll wince. But tell me I'm stupid, and I'll go to any length to prove you wrong. So there you have it! Now you know my reason for writing obscure manuscripts, professing daily before a classroom full of incredulous students, and attending school forever. The cat's out of the bag.

The second lesson about stigmas lies within this insight about myself. I asked earlier: If the parent protects Jimmy by stigmatizing Suzie and if the State protects the public by marking the criminal, then who do we protect when we stigmatize others for simply being themselves? The answer, more often than not, is ourselves.[12] *We stigmatize others to protect ourselves.*

Take my case, for example. I don't want to be thought of as ignorant. I want, instead, to put as much distance as possible between myself and stupidity. Now, what better way to accomplish that goal than to point out the stupidity of others? Every time I say—in public or to myself—"what a silly comment," I'm saying as well, "I wouldn't make such a ridiculous statement." By lowering others, then, I'm lifting myself up. I'm making myself appear intelligent by demeaning the intelligence of others.[13]

The issue, then, is not simply that I must protect others from error. Nor is the problem merely one of stereotyping a person on the basis of certain behavioral traits. At bottom, the problem of stigmatizing others lies within myself. My own ambition. My own desire to be thought of as someone important or admirable. My own compulsion for status and prestige. My own inability to be satisfied with myself. My own insecurity. My own pride. My own sin. The tragedy of stigmas is that they not only mask as a good thing, but they also cover a multitude of sins.

## Lessons for Victims of Stigmas

But what about those who are the objects of stigmas? It's good to understand why someone stigmatizes others, but doesn't such an analysis miss the point a bit? After all, the ones who deserve our compassion are not the people who stigmatize but their victims. What about them? What are the redemptive possibilities for the victims of stigmas?

We looked first at those who stigmatize for a reason: Victims will never begin the process of redemption unless they first begin to understand the people who are the source of their problem. That will not be easy. Those who are experiencing rejection due to stigma are prone to focus on themselves. That focus may take the form of self-incrimination, self-pity, or self-defense. In any case, victims see the stigmatizer as one who deserves to be ignored or blamed, but not understood. Such a response makes sense. But it's not helpful.

Victims who are able to shift the focus from themselves to the stigmatizers, however, will discover some interesting things. Most importantly, they'll learn that stigmatizers are also victims. Why? Because if our analysis of stigmas has any merit, then it clearly demonstrates that the stigmatizer is awash in a sea of self-deceit, ignorance, and sin. Especially sin. Though stigmas wrap themselves in the garb of righteous indignation, they merely hide a heart of selfish motives. And though the world may care little about the consequences of such attitudes, the Christian has no such option. We know the results of sin, and we ought to be as worried as hell about them.

Understanding stigmatizers, however, does more than give us a bit of sympathy for them. It also helps us deal with the effects of stigma. To see this, let's return to the experience of my black friend at prep school. When he went through his first year of rejection, it decimated his ego. When he returned home the next summer, people noticed that something had happened. He had changed. He had become more quiet and reclusive.

His lifelong pastor noticed his behavior, suspected its source, and made a point to spend some time with him. The pastor gave my friend the following advice: "First," he said, "I want you to understand that you are the victim of bigotry and prejudice. Second, you need to realize that your classmates at school are also the victims of bigotry and prejudice. And, third, before you go back to school next fall, you'd better believe God loves you." The advice seemed strange at first, but it eventually changed my friend's life.

Why? Because the pastor's advice was full of truth. First, it confronted my friend with the source of his stigma (i.e. bigotry and prejudice). That defined the problem for him and released him from the prison of self-incrimination. Whatever deficiencies and weaknesses he possessed—and he knew he had his share—they weren't the primary reason for his problem. He didn't need to go through the next year, therefore, with endless self-doubt. His pastor had provided him with an honest assessment of the situation, and he believed it. Relief.

Second, the pastor's advice confronted him with the depths of human depravity. Sin. At first blush, that might not seem obvious. But how is it that we can come to see an enemy as a victim? Only when we understand that the enemy's efforts lead to his or her own downfall. The stigmatizer reaps the whirlwind, not the harvest. Hatred built on ignorance and pride leads only to further hatred. The stigmatizer may feel a sense of victory, but nothing close to joy.

It took my friend some time to understand this because the stigmas had hurt him deeply. But when the truth of the pastor's advice penetrated his heart, the sting of the stigma started to ease. When his classmates ignored him, he began to see it as their loss, not his. When his friends acted strangely around him, he chalked it up to ignorance and made it his mission to give them a primer on black culture.

Most importantly, however, the pastor's advice confronted my friend with his greatest need. He felt rejected. Unloved. Forsaken. That is why his stigma seemed so unbearable and his stay at school not worth the pain. In his forsakenness, he had come to doubt himself as well as his Creator.

But out of his forsakenness came this startling conclusion: He believed in God's love only as long as he was surrounded by the love of others. In the warm embrace of his family and friends, it was easy to believe that God loved him. But sitting in the isolation of his dorm room,

God's love seemed far removed. He was, he decided, a fair-weather believer. And he determined to change. The reality of God's love didn't have the effect my friend assumed it would. It didn't make him need friends any less. It didn't eliminate the pain of rejection. But it did enable him to love those whom God placed along the way. And that changed his life. He found that some who had previously ignored him now responded with interest. Not all, but some. He discovered that some who acted strangely before, increasingly relaxed around him. Not all, but some. Over a period of time, then, he found that out of his love for others, he slowly acquired a community of his own. And, thus, he rediscovered what he thought God had asked him to forfeit in prep school: the love of God returning to him through the lives of other believers.

## Conclusion

My friend's story had a happy ending. I wish that was always the case. I wish that all victims of stigma would be able to find loyal companions. But that doesn't always happen. I had another friend, no, an acquaintance—who lost the use of her limbs through a disease. She was confined to a wheel chair. People began to treat her differently. She became bitter, despondent, and paranoid. When she moved into my social orbit, I couldn't bring myself to build a relationship with her. A few years later she died, without a friend in the world. Alone.

I mention her case, not because I feel guilty (though I do), but to remind us of the tragedy of stigmatizing. What my friend did at prep school is unusual. Most people are not up to it.

Sometimes the victim's circumstances make finding friends very difficult. That was the message of *The Elephant Man*. Those of us who are not victims of stigmas need to hear that message. We need to think about it before we paste labels on others. We need to consider it before we close off our world from peculiarity. We need to act on it and begin the process of breaking down artificial barriers—in family, church, school, neighborhood, business, and government—that keep us from seeing one another as God's image bearers.

But there is another message, found in God's Word. And the message is especially appropriate for those of us who find ourselves locked in the grip of a stigma and rejection. The message is that we are the fruit of our Creator's imagination. He made us. Wonderfully. And because of Jesus Christ, he sees us the way he made us, not the way others see us. He loves us. And that love is available to us, just as it was to my friend in prep school. If we recognize and accept that love, as did he, it will change our lives. Forever.

# 3

## *Pain: Rejection by God*

━━━━━━━━━━━━━━━━━━━━━━━━━━━━━━━━━━━━━━━━━━━━━━━━

*Lord, it is dark.*
*Lord, are you here in my darkness?*
*Where are you, Lord?*
*Do you love me still?*
*Or have I wearied you?*
*Lord, answer.*
*Answer!*
*It is dark.*

Michel Quoist, *Prayers*

Like everyone else, I grew up with pain. I experienced the same bruises—to body and ego—that other children experienced, and I was exposed to the same kind of hurt when friends or family members died. But it wasn't until I had a child of my own that I understood the full impact of the problem of pain.

One incident stands out in my mind. When our oldest daughter was only two, we moved to western New York where I was newly employed. In the midst of unloading the van, one of my colleagues invited us over for lunch. We promptly accepted the invitation and walked the short distance to his home. When we stepped into his house, however, we were greeted by the sight of his four-year-old daughter, lying on the floor, babbling incoherently, flailing her arms in the air, and pounding her head on the carpet. I immediately assumed she was having some kind of a seizure, but I was surprised to see that my colleague wasn't a bit perturbed by her behavior. Instead, he simply stepped up behind her and gently pulled her into his embrace. After hugging her affectionately, he looked up at us and said, "I'd like to introduce you to my daughter, Maya."

In due time we learned Maya's story. She had come into the world as a healthy, robust, little baby. She was the first child in the family and the apple of her parents' eyes. One day, however, she came down with a fever— not unusual for young children—but this fever didn't act normally. Instead of stopping at 103° or 104°, it continued to climb. And before it had reached its zenith, it had permanently damaged Maya's brain, leaving her helpless and totally incapacitated. In a matter of minutes their beautiful little daughter had been reduced to a vegetable.

It is impossible for a parent to witness such a scene without thinking of one's own child, and in my mind's eye, the image of my own daughter Heather became larger than life. Maya was his Heather. All of the love and affection that I had for Heather, he had for Maya. All of the hopes and dreams for the future. All of the fond remembrances of the past. All of the longings and joys that were mine as a parent, were his as well. And now, there he was, sitting on the floor with his arms wrapped around a promise—a promise taken away only moments after it had been uttered, a promise never to be fulfilled.

The pain of the moment was unbearable. And, in fact, in order to cope I had to erase Heather from my mind and pretend that Maya was a stranger. But Maya was no stranger. She was my daughter and the feelings of her parents were mine as well. And with those feelings came one irrepressible question: "Why, God? Why did you allow this to happen?" And when there is no answer, a second question comes fast on its heels: "Are you listening to me, God? Do you care? Are you even there?"

Most modern Christians are aware of what has sometimes been called the *problem of pain*.[1] In simple terms, it raises the question: How can a good God allow so much pain and suffering in the world? How can a merciful God allow babies to die of painful diseases? How can a just God permit the Hitlers and Stalins of the world to murder millions of men, women, and children? Or, turning to the Bible itself, how can a loving God allow his good and faithful servant Job to be ruined by the Evil One?

## An Undeserved Pain

Job is an interesting example, I think, because it's hard to imagine a more undeserved pain than the one he suffered. All of us, of course, have endured pain. Some of us have had to put up with long bouts of sickness, or we've agonized through the miseries of others. But few adults have undergone a tragedy like Job's, and even fewer have been as blameless.

The Bible doesn't tell us too much about Job, but three things in particular are worth noting. First, he lived. That is, he was a real man, full of the humanity that characterizes us all. Second, he was a wealthy man, with abundant capital, numerous helpers, and a large family. All of these, by the way, he considered gifts from God (Job 1:21). Third, and most important, he was blameless and upright. This doesn't mean he was without sin, but it indicates that he was an obedient servant of the Lord, a man who fled from sin and honored God in his behavior and attitudes. In righteousness, we are told, Job had no equal (Job 1:8).

What happens to this man, however, is hard to believe. His story (like ours) begins in heaven. There we find Satan sneaking into God's presence on the coattails of other angels. The Lord spies him and asks, "Where have you come from?" The Lord asks the question not because he doesn't know but in order to remind Satan of his place. In bragging fashion, Satan responds, "From roaming through the earth and going back and forth in it" (1:7). A rough paraphrase might be, "I have come from the earth, Lord. That's my place. You may have created it, but now it belongs to me. I roam at will. And the people fear me, not you!"

Instead of throwing Satan out on his ear, the Lord counters Satan's boast with evidence. "Have you considered my servant Job?" he asks. "There is no one on earth like him; he is blameless and upright, a man who fears God and shuns evil" (1:8). Though the evidence is undeniable, Satan discounts its importance. He claims that Job is following the Lord only because the Lord has been such a marvelous Sugar Daddy, giving Job whatever his heart desires. Take away Job's blessings, Satan claims, and "he will surely curse you to your face" (1:11). Knowing Job, the Lord says, "Very well, then, everything he has is in your hands" (1:12).

We all know what happens after that. In one day, Job discovers that his means of support has disappeared and his children have all been killed. When he refuses to curse God for this calamity, God allows Satan to strike again, this time covering Job with painful, ugly sores. In short, Job loses everything of value except his life, his wife, and his friends—and their value is questionable. "In all this," however, "Job did not sin in what he said" (2:10). Instead, he asks his nagging wife, "Shall we accept good from God, and not trouble" (2:10). And to his Lord he confesses, "Naked I came from my mother's womb, and naked I will depart. The Lord gave and the Lord has taken away; may the name of the Lord be praised" (1:21).

Up to this point, the story of Job is a marvelous tale of faith. Job has suffered an unbelievable tragedy, and yet his faith in God has not been shaken. The story of Job is not over, however. Indeed, the human battle has only just begun. Now Job must *live* with his tragedy. That means not only enduring physical pain but also attempting to make sense out of an ongoing, senseless tragedy. As is so often the case, it is in living with tragedy that the problem of pain becomes unbearable. Certainly that was the case for Job.

For at least a week, Job mourns his losses and holds his tongue. Finally, however, he unleashes his anguish in the presence of three friends who have ostensibly come to sympathize with him. His basic question is "Why?" Why did this calamity happen? Why did God allow it to happen? Why, if God knew it was going to happen, did he ever permit Job to be born? Why, now that it has happened, doesn't God let Job die? And, maybe most perplexing of all, "Why do the wicked live on, growing old and increasing in power," (21:7) while righteous Job lies writhing in misery and pain?

To these questions, Job's friends have an answer. It's the only theologically correct answer they can come up with. "Who, being innocent," asks Eliphaz, "has ever perished? Where were the upright ever destroyed? As I have observed, those who plow evil and those who sow trouble reap it" (4:7–8).

Eliphaz asserts a fundamental principle: people get what they deserve. If Job were innocent, he wouldn't be having these troubles. The conclusion, then, is that Job must be paying the price for some secret sin. "He who sows wickedness reaps trouble" (Prov. 22:8). It's a conclusion for which there is ample biblical support.[2]

Despite that fact, the reasoning of Job's friends is seriously flawed. Job, remember, is innocent. God himself has called Job blameless. Job, as well, maintains his own innocence, even under the incessant attacks of his friends.

But Job has a serious problem. If he is innocent, then why is he being afflicted? Job has no answer to that question. He is left, then, with friends who don't understand him and a God who will not explain his behavior.

Job concludes, "I cry out to you, O God, but you do not answer; I stand up, but you merely look at me. You turn on me ruthlessly; with the might of your hand you attack me. You snatch me up and drive me before the wind; you toss me about in the storm. I know you will bring me down to death, to the place appointed for all the living. Surely no one lays a hand on a broken man when he cries for help in his distress. Have I not wept for those in trouble? Has not my soul grieved for the poor? Yet when I hoped for good, evil came; when I looked for light, then came darkness" (30:20–27).

Job. God's loyal servant. Groping around in the dark. Without answers. Lost in the forsakenness of unjustified pain.

## An Unavailable God

Why does Job feel forsaken? Not for reasons typical of forsaken people. Job was not lacking in company, for example. His wife, nagging though she may have been, was still at his side. His friends, poor advisers to be sure, didn't desert him in his time of need. Indeed, before they counseled him, they sat with him silently for seven days. They understood, in other words, his deep grief as well as his need for quiet consolation. Thus, though Job had lost his wealth and his children, he hadn't lost all companionship. Job had not suffered the rejection of friends.

Nevertheless, Job felt rejected. Not by people. But by the sovereign God of the universe. In the jargon of theology, Job was a Calvinist. He knew who controlled the destinies of nations as well as people. He knew that nothing could happen without the Lord's consent and that God himself, therefore, had allowed this terrible tragedy to occur. What he didn't understand was *why* God had allowed it.

Job had always found God faithful in the past. He had learned that if he honored God with his life, God would bless his living. Now, however, all that seemed to change. He continued to trust in God's provision, but God was no longer providing. He continued to play the game of life by the Book, but God no longer seemed interested in abiding by his own rules. Job was suffering a grievous injustice, and the Lord of mercy seemed not to care. Job's pain, then, was more than painful. It was evidence of divine rejection.

It is hard to think of a rejection more total than that which comes from God's absence. When we are rejected by others because we carry a stigma, we can rest assured that the Lord will never reject us for such a reason. But what comfort is there for those who feel they've been abandoned by God?

And yet, that is precisely how the problem of pain makes you feel. You pray and pray that God will heal your dying child, and yet the disease continues to spread. You plead with God to send the rains to Ethiopia, but the land remains parched, and people die by the thousands. You beg the Lord to heal a broken relationship, but the relationship remains unraveled. For ten years, you praise God for the ministry of your pastor, only to discover that he's been carrying on an affair with the church secretary the whole time.

And in your pain, you do the only thing you can. You cry out to God with questions like Job's. Why, Lord? Why, in heaven's name, do you let such things happen? How, in the name of justice, can you allow the Evil One to have his way like that? Why don't you respond to my pleas, Lord? Why do you keep silent in the face of such wrongs? Are you listening to me, Lord, or are my words bouncing off heaven's door? Why have I been abandoned in my time of greatest need?

Make no mistake, these are tough questions. They were difficult for Job. They were difficult for me when I was confronted with Maya. And they remain difficult not only for me, but for anyone who believes in a God of love. They aren't hard to ask, certainly. It's the answers we find problematic. Good ones don't seem to exist! Or if they exist, they seem neither good nor satisfactory. The questions are disturbing precisely because they come to us so often, and yet they come without solid answers. Why is that? And what are we to do with these questions that rain on us without mercy or answers?

## Questioning the Answers

Once we have concluded that a pain is undeserved, the "why" question is nearly irresistible.[3] The moment we begin coming up with definitive answers, however, we always seem to run amuck. The reason? If pain is undeserved, then its existence can't be blamed on the one who feels it.[4] As a result, the focus of such questions always shifts away from the one in pain and toward the One who has power over pain. In other words, this question always puts the spotlight on God. And he is the One about whom we begin to speculate.

*One solution to the problem of pain is to conclude that God is too weak to help suffering people.* This, it seems to me, is how Rabbi Kushner deals with the problem in his book, *When Bad Things Happen to Good People.* This approach presumes that a God of love could not tolerate undeserved human pain. Such misery exists, then, not because God allows it to exist, but because he is unable to do anything about it. God would like nothing more than to relieve us of our misery, but his hands are tied. The conditions prevent his intervention. In this approach, God remains compassionate and loving, but he is something less than the all-powerful sovereign that Jews and Christians have always believed him to be.

*Another solution to the problem of pain is to doubt the goodness of God.* This is the assumption made in Greek mythology, where evil exists not only because the gods can't prevent it but also because sometimes they don't want to.[5] The gods' motives, like those of humans, are mixed. Modern Christians, of course, are rarely tempted to think of God in such anthropomorphic terms. But we can be tempted to believe that God is not as loving as the Bible asserts. Especially in the case of undeserved pain, it's easy for us to imagine that he is too busy to notice or more than just a tad hard. How else could he passively endure something like the holocaust, we ask? And suddenly, the God who describes himself as Love Incarnate is something less than loving.

*A third solution to the problem is to conclude that God doesn't exist.*[6] The proponents of this solution argue that a good God couldn't endure undeserved pain. Therefore, such a god doesn't exist. This is a "clean" approach to the problem, since it doesn't attempt to muddy up traditional Christian doctrines. It simply breaks with the tradition altogether. But this solution has the disadvantage of failing to deal with the original problem. It's hard to see how believing that God doesn't exist would enable one to feel less lonely or less abandoned. Indeed, atheists solve the problem of pain by affirming their cosmic alienation. A bold declaration, but an odd approach to the problem of forsakenness.

That problem is not the atheist's alone, moreover. None of the other solutions to the problem of pain deal effectively with forsakenness either. To believe that God is weak, for example, may preserve God's compassionate character, but it hardly enables one to feel less forsaken: To move from the acknowledgment that God isn't helping, to the assumption that he *can't* help, is not especially comforting to me. Similarly, to believe God is less compassionate than I am might explain his willingness to tolerate my pain, but it hardly makes me feel closer to him. Whether he is lacking in power or compassion, the bottom line is that God has left me alone because his character is flawed. That's not only heretical. It's profoundly depressing.

There are, certainly, many other ways to handle the problem of pain, including the denial that it even exists.[7] My point is not to create a smorgasbord of possibilities, but to show the risky nature of the enterprise. For the Christian, the problem of pain almost always becomes a question about the nature of God. Such questions are certainly legitimate, but biblical answers are not necessarily forthcoming. Indeed, while the Bible reveals much about the character of our Lord, there remains much we neither know nor understand. That is especially the case when we come to the problem of pain. When Job asked God why he was allowing Job to suffer, he had more of a right to the question than any human I know. And yet God chose not to answer. Instead he responded to Job's question with one of his own: "Where were you when I laid the earth's foundation?" (Job 38:4). It's a sobering question. And one consistent with a God who says of himself, "I am who I am" (Exod. 3:14).

## Questioning the Problem

So what are we to do? We seem to have a question for which there are no good answers. Does that mean we are stuck with a forsakenness for which there is no cure? What do we do with the question? And how do we cope with the pain?

When a question consistently leads to dead ends—or worse—the question itself merits some inspection. And, in this case, I think it would be helpful to look at the problem of pain sociologically. From that perspective, the productive inquiry is not, "Why would a good God allow the innocent to suffer?" but rather "Why do we ask such questions?" Or, putting it more precisely, why do *we,* as modern citizens of the industrial West, raise the problem of pain?

That may seem like an odd question, especially to those who have assumed that people have always had a burning interest in the problem of pain. In fact, however, the problem of pain has not been of equal concern to all people. Indeed, it's only in the last two or three hundred years that the problem of pain has become a central issue for the Christian community.[8] Now, please, don't misunderstand. The problem of pain has always been a concern for humanity. It was certainly an issue for Job, and he lived quite some time ago. What is different about us, however, is that it seems to be a *central* problem in our thinking, whereas in the past it was only one of a number of theological issues available for discussion.

The question, then, is why are we in the modern Western world so enamored by this particular issue? Why is it so important to us? Why does it occupy such a central place in our thinking, and why does it give us such a headache? Sociologists would debate the answers, of course, but let me give you my answer: The problem of pain is of central concern in the modern West not because we are an especially bright or compassionate people but because we are an especially wealthy people. It is our bounty, not our brilliance that pushes this question to center stage.

The fact that we are wealthy, by historical and global standards, is something that needs no explanation. In the past, few have been as prosperous as we are, and even then, they were always a minority within their own society. Even today, few outside the West live as we do, and again, they are a minority within their own nations.[9]

What needs to be explained is not the fact of our wealth but its relationship to the problem of pain.

For the poor, the central philosophical problem is not the existence of pain but the presence of joy. The impoverished, you see, don't expect the world to be wonderful. The world for them is a hard place, where infants die more often than survive, where adults live with chronic illnesses and persistent pain, and where an unsatisfied stomach is routine. In such a world, pain is not a surprise. It's a fact of life. The inexplicable thing is that, in such a world, there is also joy, beauty, and pleasure. *That* is the problem. Why is there joy in the midst of despair? Why is there beauty in the midst of so much ugliness? How can there be pleasure even in the pit of despair? And for most of the poor, throughout most of recorded history, the answer has pointed them beyond themselves, toward other worlds, where there is a Greater Good than the one they are now enjoying.

The wealthy have a different problem, however. They have come to *expect* good times. They have learned that life is to be enjoyed. In the modern world, for example, the middle class is encouraged to "go for the gusto," to enjoy the good life. Often, this is coupled with an expectation that hard work necessarily results in a successful life. Thus, modern, middle-class Christians come to life with the assumption of Eliphaz, "You sow what you reap." The good life, we believe, is there for the taking. God is a good God. He has put his good creation at our disposal. It's simply our responsibility to take it and enjoy it. God wants us to be happy and enjoy his bounty.

The problem, of course, is that life doesn't always work out that way. Sin pervades our existence. And pain isn't the domain only of the poor. Wealth may put off pain for a while and mollify its effects, but sooner or later, pain will intrude into the lives of the wealthy. And when it does, it's a shock and a terrible disappointment. It throws into question all of one's assumptions. About life. Its purposes. And its Lord. "How could God allow this to happen?" we say. "I thought God was a good God? I thought he wanted only the best for me? I thought he promised to bless those who were obedient to his commands? What has happened to my assumptions? What has happened to my God?"

*The problem of pain, then, is of central importance to us precisely because we don't expect it.* One might say that we have come to take God's blessings for granted. They are our expectations. When they don't come our way, however, or when an unjustified pain comes instead, we're surprised. We are crushed. The sad thing, of course, is that because we've learned to expect happiness, we moderns are no longer able to be surprised by joy. We are surprised by pain, instead, and that is a surprise far more difficult to take. Or explain.

## Questioning the Source

The connection between affluence and the problem of pain is all the more intriguing, I think, when we remember the reason for pain in the first place. Biblically speaking, pain is a product of God's mercy. That may seem like another odd assertion from an increasingly odd author, but I believe it stands the test of scrutiny.

Pain, remember, is a consequence of the Fall. It was through Adam and Eve's sin that pain and suffering entered the human domain. That is easy to remember.

What is harder to recall, however, is that the proper penalty for sin is death. And because God is a righteous and holy God, he tolerates no sin. Thus, when he put Adam and Eve into the Garden, he did two things. First, he made it as easy as possible for them not to sin, giving them everything in the Garden except the fruit of just one tree. But second, he warned them of the consequences of sin—death.

We all know what happened. They ate the fruit, and as a consequence, we all bear the effects of sin, including death. But now note this. Had God dealt with Adam and Eve efficiently and in accordance with his own standards, they would have died immediately, and the human race would've come to a swift end. But God chose to deal with them mercifully, not in relation to his justice, but in terms of his grace. Adam and Eve lived to experience the joys (and sorrows) of marriage, children, work, and so on. More amazingly, God didn't simply give them a reprieve. He also began the process of reconciling himself to his creation, offering redemption from sin and a renewed relationship to him. And why would God do this? Because he didn't want anyone to perish (2 Peter 3:9). Because God is a God of mercy.

We live with pain as well as pleasure, then, not because God is lacking in compassion, but precisely the opposite. It was out of his compassion that he spared us. And it is out of his compassion that he forestalls his justice even now.

The bottom line is that God loves us. Inspired by that love, he has acted in the spirit of the father of the Prodigal Son. We are the ones who said, "Let us live apart from you and enjoy your creation and squander our inheritance." He is the One who let us go, enduring our abuse of his world and our consequent pain, because he looks forward to the day of our homecoming—that day of reconciliation, when he will kill the fatted calf and we will feast with him forever.

## Conclusion

Until that time, however, some of us will endure the forsakenness of pain. It's a genuine feeling, but it's based upon a genuine lie. That God allows suffering there can be no doubt. That he doesn't explain his every action none can deny. But to these facts must be added the most pervasive truth of all, a truth seared into history at the Cross and demonstrated for all time in the life of Christ: Our God is a God of love who "heals the brokenhearted and binds up their wounds" (Ps. 147:3) In our pain, we may feel many things. But we are not forsaken.

None of this may make pain any easier to take, by the way. The image of Maya, limp and contorted in her father's embrace, still brings tears to my eyes. As well it should. Maya, and the millions of others like her, remind us that something is not right with our world. That things are askew. Confronted with such a scene, everything in us wants to cry out, "No! This is wrong! Something needs to be changed!" Such scenes bear testimony to a fundamental flaw in the human condition, as clear an indication of Adam and Eve's sin as ever there could be.

But the picture of Maya is not complete if all we see is a child lying on the floor, disfigured by the effects of the Fall. For the picture also includes a father, bruised but not defeated, who does not rush out of the room in horror nor abandon his broken creation. Instead, the father drops down to the level of his child, joining her on the floor that has become her home, and pulls her into his warm embrace. And to the multitudes of heavenly hosts, looking on in disbelief, he simply says, "I'd like to introduce you to my child, Maya. I love her. And I will not let her go."

In the end, then, pain remains a mercy. A severe mercy, to be sure, but a mercy nevertheless.[10] For pain is a reminder not only of evil but also of the obstinate love of our heavenly Father. A love that would not abandon us, even when we deserved to be abandoned. From a God who would not let us go, even when we were bound and determined to live without him. Our problem is not that we don't understand pain. It's that we can't comprehend God's mercy. We can't imagine a love so great that it is willing to endure us.

When we suffer, then, we should do more than simply feel pain. We ought to marvel at the patience of a gracious God as well. And know that we have not been forsaken.

# REDEEMING THE EXPERIENCE
# OF LOSS

It's easy to understand why we feel forsaken if someone rejects us. There is nothing ambiguous about the words, "Get out of my life!" But it's important to understand that forsakenness is a perception as much as an event. More precisely, forsakenness is an interpretation of the meaning of events. As a result, we can feel abandoned when we lose a significant relationship, even though that other person has not rejected us. The loss of a person close to us, regardless of the reasons for it, can lead to a profound sense of abandonment.

Chapters 4 and 5 will consider two different types of loss. The first is the most apparent, for it involves the feeling of loss that accompanies the death of a close friend or relative. It is most apparent because it is universal; we all will have to cope with grief at some point in our lives. The second type of loss is not so obvious and, on the surface, may even seem a bit odd. This loss involves the relationship between knowledge and our sense of God's presence in our lives. Strange or not, this loss too can lead to a profound sense of abandonment—as well as the possibility of redemption.

# 4

## *Grief: Loss of Others*

‖‖‖‖‖‖‖‖‖‖‖‖‖‖‖‖‖‖‖‖‖‖‖‖‖‖‖‖‖‖‖‖‖‖‖‖‖‖‖‖‖‖‖‖‖‖‖‖‖‖‖‖‖‖‖‖‖‖‖‖‖‖‖‖‖‖‖‖‖‖‖‖‖‖‖‖‖‖‖‖‖‖‖‖‖‖

*How long will you forget me, Lord? Forever?*
*How long will you look the other way*
*    when I am in need?*
*How long must I be hiding daily [grief]*
*    in my heart?*
*Answer me, O Lord my God;*
*    give me light in my darkness lest I die.*
*                                    Psalm 13:1–2, 3 (TLB)*

For many of us, our most common image of abandonment involves the grieving family member left behind by the death of a loved one. We think perhaps of the elderly widow, standing beside her husband's grave, pondering the loss of a fifty- or sixty-year companion. The image is an appropriate one, I think. For it's hard to imagine a more archetypal experience of forsakenness than the loneliness that results from the loss of a lifelong spouse.

Regardless of how affectionate a couple might be, when they've been together for a long period of time, they establish a rhythm to their relationship. Though to the outsider the rhythm may sound like the steady beat of a single drum, in fact, it results from the coordinated efforts of two interdependent percussionists. When one drummer dies, the other is left trying either to play both drums at the same time or to make one drum sound like two. It's a futile effort, of course, and the result is a life that seems off-beat and unfulfilled. The old rhythm is gone, and no new syncopation is satisfactory.

## A Grief Observed[1]

It would be wrong, however, to assume that death generates forsakenness only when it separates lifelong companions. I was struck by this when my own father died. At the time of his death, I was thirty years old. I had been married for nine years, lived 3,000 miles to the east, and had two children of my own. I had, in other words, established an independent, nuclear family, physically separated from the family of my youth. And yet, when my father died, I was overcome not only with reasonable feelings of grief but also with a surprising sense of abandonment as well. Why was that?

A full answer, I suspect, would require a lifetime of reflection. But the simple answer is this. When I was growing up, my father was the most responsible member of our family. By that, I don't mean that he was the only person in the family who possessed a sense of integrity. I mean, rather, that my father was the one who was ultimately responsible for the welfare of the family. He assumed that position both by custom and by personality. On the one hand, he was the product of a rural, patriarchal tradition. He was a farmer, the only bread-winner in the family, and he took that status seriously. On the other hand, he had a very prudent disposition. He was the conservative one in the family, and we all relied on his wisdom. It was in character, therefore, for him to be a bit cautious, and he used this trait to hold in the reins on the aberrant energies of the rest of us.

Especially mine. When I was young, for example, I was prone to be rather argumentative about things. If I'd been treated unjustly, I wasn't afraid to let everyone know about it. When my interpretation of justice was disputed, moreover, I would argue my case with intensity. My father, however, didn't like wordy argumentation. He enjoyed a good debate, certainly, but not one that was loud or overly personal. Consequently, he took it upon himself to restrain my argumentative nature. His approach was maddeningly simple. The moment I began to raise my voice during a dispute, he would calmly interrupt with the words: "The argument is over. You lost." Then he would walk away. He did this because, as he told me many times, when one loses one's temper, one has effectively lost the debate, regardless of the merits of one's case. Needless to say, I was frustrated with this maneuver, especially because it came just as I was getting into my argument. Needless to say, as well, I soon learned to keep a cool head during disputes.

It may seem odd to reflect on this incident in relation to my father's death, since it was, after all, a negative learning experience for me. Nevertheless, it was a learning experience in keeping with my father's role within the family. And he played his role with great effect. I came to depend upon it. Indeed, it was only after I left the nest, that I came to realize how well he played it and how much I depended upon it for my own survival. Though he was no longer living with me, his voice was still buried deep within my consciousness. And every time my temperature began to climb near the boiling point—whether over a grade in graduate school or an argumentative student in class or an insulting colleague at a professional conference—I could hear my father getting ready to say, "The argument is over. You lost."

Those are words I will never hear him say again. More precisely, that is a role my father can no longer play in my own life. It was the loss of that role, more than anything else, that struck me after his death. Oh, yes, his words were still etched firmly in my mind. And they will continue to have their effect, especially when I'm in the midst of heated debate. Death can't take that away from me. But there will never be any new words added to the advice. What I have are memories. Important and powerful as they may be, they are mere figments of the real thing. The living, dynamic presence of my father, however, is gone. The possibility of calling him up to ask for advice is gone. The knowledge that he will be there in time of trouble is gone. The satisfaction of his silent approval is gone. The comfort that comes from being under a responsible authority is gone.

### Learning from Grief

The abandonment I felt after my father's death, I suspect, is not unusual. With death comes loss, and unless one is anxious to be rid of a relationship, death tears at the social fabric of our lives. Indeed, even when we lose people whom we find obnoxious or irritating, we may still feel loss because they too are a part of our relational network. We don't have to like people to miss them.

The degree to which we feel loss, however, will be affected by the conditions under which we experience it. A number of researchers, for example, have noted that grief is more likely to be intense when associated with a sudden, *unanticipated* death.[2] The accidental death of a young person, for example, is more likely to cause a deep sense of loss than the death of someone who has undergone a prolonged, excruciating illness. Thus, the grief I experienced at the loss of my cousin Paul was more intense than the grief I felt after my grandfather died, even though I loved them both. Paul's death, remember, resulted from an automobile accident. It was sudden and unexpected. My grandfather's death, however, was *anticipated*; he died after a twenty-year struggle with Parkinson's disease. Thus, even though I experienced grief at grandpa's death, it was not as powerful or acute as my reaction when I learned the news about Paul.

One obvious reason for this is that we feel a certain amount of injustice with the sudden death of a young person; they're too young to die, we think, and their death seems unfair. Upon reflection, however, it's clear that much more is going on than righteous indignation. First, when we know that someone is going to die, we have a chance to prepare for it. In a sense, we can begin the process of grief before the actual death takes place. That may or may not be good, but it does allow us to think about the death beforehand and to consider its consequences.[3] This gives us a greater sense of control over events and the possibility of planning for the death and its aftermath. Not everyone will take advantage of this possibility, of course. Some will deny that death is imminent, and the greater their denial, the greater their sense of loss. Those who experience the sudden death of a friend or loved one, however, don't even have the possibility to prepare.[4]

Second, anticipated death is usually a little less

frightening,[5] and in some cases, that death actually may be a relief. My wife's grandmother, for example, spent the last few years of her life in a medical facility, unable to feed herself or communicate with others. She was merely surviving. For most of her life, however, she had been an active, energetic woman who enjoyed living. When she was in her eighties, for example, she had the gumption to fly across the country and spend three months with us in a two-bedroom apartment. She did this not for a vacation but in order to take the day shift with our newborn baby. It was extremely painful, then, to see this once-vibrant person vegetate in a hospital bed. As a result, when she "went home to be with the Lord," it was a great relief, not only to us, but I'm sure for her as well.[6]

Compare her death, however, with the deaths of two of our church's young people who were killed in a car accident on their way to college. Imagine the parents' shock and grief to lose their only children in the same accident. In an instant, they lost the two most important people in their lives. Without preparation, they were severed from future hopes and present responsibilities by an event that was previously unimaginable. They didn't love their children any more than we loved grandma. They certainly had the same hope of an eternal destiny. Yet, my friends' loss was incalculably greater. Why? Because grandma's death was an expected, understandable conclusion to her life, while their children's deaths were an unfathomable interruption in the life of the entire family.

Other factors can make an anticipated death more manageable, of course. If we know that someone is likely to die, for example, we have the chance to talk about unresolved matters. When there is a sudden death, however, survivors are sometimes left with unexpiated guilt.[7] They may wish they could have asked for—or offered—forgiveness about some previous harm. Or they may simply wish they had unearthed feelings that previously had remained dormant. After my father's stroke, for example, one of the first things I did was to write him a letter in which I told him how much I appreciated and loved him. Though at the time I didn't realize it, I know now that I was anticipating his death; I needed to tell him something about which I felt deeply but, for a number of reasons, had previously found difficult to articulate.[8] Being able to communicate with him at that time, then, was important to me. Had he died suddenly, however, I would have been robbed of that opportunity—and I would have felt much worse about my loss.

The difference in our response to anticipated and unanticipated death is important to remember, especially when we consider grief in the context of modern society. Compared to our ancestors, we are a people unaccustomed to death. In part, that is because it occurs less often.[9] Fewer of us are likely to die during childbirth, for one thing, but we are also less likely to die while growing up or during midlife. What this means, of course, is that death is not the same kind of everyday reality for us that it was—and is—in pre- and newly industrializing societies.[10]

And yet, death continues to happen. Though we live longer, we will all die. The fact of death remains. This means that the modern approach to death is not simply a response to changing facts. It also entails a different attitude about these facts. As death has become less familiar, as modern medicine has given us a greater sense of control over sickness, we have assumed the right to live longer. With modernity has come the *expectation* of growing older. We talk about "life-expectancy" rates, not death-expectancy, and we assume the right to live well into our eighties and nineties. Indeed, we feel unfairly treated when "fate" cheats us of our "life rights."

This expectation, moreover, is protected by modern life. The nuclear family, for example, enables us to distance ourselves physically and emotionally from extended family members. We call them our "loved ones," and yet they are hardly a part of our lives. Our jobs, moreover, usually don't provide the context for truly close relationships. And, of course, the modern church, with its transitory parishioners, doesn't offer many enduring relationships either. As a result, many of our acquaintances are based on only limited contact; we know people with our minds, but their lives hardly impinge upon our own.[11] Thus, even when people we know "pass away," we simply don't feel the impact. We may send a card. We may even go to the funeral. But our lives aren't interrupted.

Until, that is, a truly close friend or family member dies. Then, suddenly, we are massively confronted with death. Having socially denied its existence, however, we aren't prepared for death when it finally happens. Having not rehearsed it often in our lives, we aren't adept at coping with its exigencies. And having other modern people around us, who are themselves desperately trying to avoid the reality of death, we may receive little long-term support in our moment of need. By virtue of our approach to death, then, every grief is unanticipated. We moderns set ourselves up for the feelings of forsakenness.

## Lessons for Prevention

Our sense of loss varies with the type of grief we experience. That, it seems to me, is the message of the last few pages. The closer the companion, the more unanticipated the death, the less social support in our grief, the more "modern" our context—all these factors will tend to heighten our sense of loss and the resulting feeling of abandonment. These are by no means the only important variables in the equation, but they are enough to digest for now.[12]

The question is, what do we learn from this? If our interest is prevention, two lessons seem fairly obvious. First, at the personal level, it is clear that we need to become more honest about the existence of death. By denying its reality, we turn every death into an unanticipated loss. That's not only unwise, but it's also unhealthy. Talking about death when it happens, preparing our estate for our own death, preparing our mind for the expected death of another, taking the time to mourn with those who mourn, reading of and listening to the grief experiences of others—these are just a few ways in which we can overcome our denial of death. We can't prevent unanticipated deaths, certainly, but we can prevent every death from affecting us like an unanticipated one.[13]

Secondly, at the social level, we need to understand the importance of developing communities where supportive, long-term relationships are the rule, not the exception. Without the context of community, we will not be in a position to help others cope with loss, and we will not experience others' comfort when we are grieving. In the modern world, the funeral is often followed by a broken heart and a lonely life. We can't prevent the broken heart, but a caring community can prevent a life devoid of meaningful relationships. Establishing such communities will not be easy, of course, since it runs counter to the societal norm. Nevertheless, for Christians who care about their neighbors and whose standards are not a matter of social convenience, it's an effort worth the price.

Yet, as I think about the loss I felt after the death of my dad, I'm struck by one thing: I felt abandoned *even though* I had learned these lessons. Whatever other forms of denial I may engage in periodically, for example, death denial is not one of them. Remember what I went through at the age of nineteen. Not only had I endured the trauma of Paul's death, but I was forced to contemplate my own. Beyond that, death had claimed my grandparents as well as close friends, one of whom was killed with all three of her children in an automobile accident. Death was no stranger to me. I knew of it. I expected it. And I understood it—to the extent that such a thing is truly understandable.

In addition, I grew up in a rather traditional community. Though we were modern Mennonites, we were Mennonites just the same. That meant I was part of a church where most people knew not only one another but also each other's parents and their parents and so on. It was the kind of church where people got into one's life as well as one's hair, and mutual aid was a matter of course. My "family" included not only parents, a brother and a sister, but also grandparents, cousins, and various assorted in-laws. We worked with one another daily, worshiped together weekly, and gathered at grandma's for chicken dinner at least twice a month. We made

Norman Rockwell's world appear urbane. We also supported one another in times of need. Though my wife and I eventually moved away from this community, its people remained a part of our hearts and consciousness. When my father died, therefore, I assumed—and received—their comfort. I did not mourn alone.

The preventive medicine, then, had been taken. I understood death, through both theory and experience, and I was surrounded by dependable relationships. And yet, I still felt a deep sense of forsakenness.

Why was that? A partial answer, I suppose, is that even in the most supportive of circumstances, death will result in a great deal of grief and loss. No matter how many arms reach out to hold you, they can't replace the arms of the one who has died. No matter how many times we rehearse our conversations and try to prepare for someone's death, there is no getting around the feeling of being left behind.

In the case of my father's death, however, there was more going on than simple grief. In facing up to my loss, I discovered some important truths—about my dad, myself, and my God.

**Lessons for Life**

Earlier I had said that my father was the responsible member of the family. When he died, however, I discovered that I had taken his responsibility for granted. That is, I just assumed that he was, and always would be, a dependable human being. My image of him assumed that he probably had started his own paper route at age two, and by kindergarten, he had been supporting his own family. I had no reason to doubt, therefore, that when he was one hundred years old, I would be in the grave, and he would still be getting up at five in the morning, successfully managing the family farm. When, therefore, at the age of fifty-seven he had a stroke and at the age of fifty-nine he died, I was dumbstruck—and felt a terrible sense of loss. The Dependable One was gone.

In my grief, then, I finally learned what I should have always known—that my father was a human being. He was not a god, and he didn't deserve to be set apart as an icon of responsibility. No doubt, he went through the same periods of silliness and senselessness that the rest of us experience. He had become responsible, not because he was born that way, but because he had determined (out of God's grace) to live that way.

By having taken his responsibility for granted, however, I had robbed him of both the credit he was due and, curiously, the chance to be a bit more irresponsible. On the one hand, had I considered him the sinner he undoubtedly was, I could have appreciated more fully the man he had become. I would've known, for example, that his responsibility didn't come easily and, more importantly, that it was a labor of love undertaken on my behalf. On the other hand, had I not taken his responsibility for granted, I might have been a bit more responsible myself and thus taken the burden off his shoulders to be responsible in my stead. I could have lightened his load, in other words, and enabled him to be a bit more easygoing.

The more general truth, of course, is that no one is a god, and we do people no favor by treating them as such. By foisting unrealistic expectations on regular people, we either pressure them to live up to our standards or force them to throw us and our unrealistic expectations out the window. The latter possibility explains why many modern superstars covet privacy; they can't possibly live up to their billing, so they periodically throw the public out of their lives by withdrawing. Fortunately, my dad didn't take that route. But he did try to live up to unrealistic expectations, I think, and that kept him from being as carefree as he might have allowed himself to be. Not only was that hard on him, but it denied me the chance to experience fully a side of him that—when it came through—was absolutely delightful.[14]

By now, it is probably obvious that I also learned something about myself. Because I took my father's responsibility for granted, I relied too much upon it. As a result, I sometimes used my father's dependable character as an excuse to be irresponsible. I don't mean by that that because my father was good, I was bad. Generally, that was not the case. I mean, rather, that because I could depend upon my father to take care of me, I didn't always use good judgment in the use of my own resources— whether in the form of mind, money, or motorcycles. As a result, it took me a long time, using much trial and error (especially error) to discover the benefits of personal responsibility.

No one should conclude from this, by the way, that my irresponsibility was my father's fault—that somehow, because he was too responsible, I turned into a jerk. That's a good modern conclusion, of course, since we like to see everything as somebody else's fault. But it's incorrect. The problem was that I had used my father's responsibility as an *excuse* to be irresponsible. I could have just as easily learned from his example and become more responsible myself. My brother and sister chose that route, but often I did not. No. The problem was mine, and that was the important truth I learned upon his death. When he died, I suddenly lost my safety net and was confronted with my true nature. That's one reason why I felt such a loss. The free ride was over. The Dependable One had left the scene. That was a frightening thing to comprehend, but it was also crucial for my own development. Because, through pain and aloneness, I had finally arrived at an important truth.

Both of these discoveries, about my dad and myself, led to one more important lesson. It was a lesson about God and my relationship to him. In my willingness to rest in the comfort of my father's dependability, I had inadvertently replaced God with my father. I don't mean, of course, that I had intellectually confused the two. My theology remained substantially orthodox during this entire period. Functionally, however, I had learned to put my ultimate trust in dad. He was the creator, sustainer, and provider, as far as I was concerned, and I learned to relate to him in that way.[15]

When my father died, however, my functional god died as well. This left a terrible void in my life—a void that should not have been there. Now please don't misunderstand this point. Grief is a perfectly proper thing for the Christian to experience, and it was overwhelmingly appropriate for me to grieve the loss of my father. It was sin that brought death into our lives, and everyone's death ought to remind us of the Fall. We were created to live, not die, and we were created to live in relationship to others. When someone dies, it is a terrible aberration of God's plan. We want to cry out "Oh God, no! This is wrong!" And, of course, it is wrong. Sin is the carrier of death, and it's the thing that condemns us to the loneliness of grief.

But in my father's death, I experienced a loss that I should not have experienced. And it was that loss that forced me to rethink my orthodoxy, and ultimately, my relationship to God. The "rethinking" process took quite a while, by the way, and it was punctuated with any number of heresies. My first reaction to the loss of my god, for example, was to attempt to be a god myself. Strange? I don't think so. You see, when my dad died, I thought I had to take his place. Just as I had perceived him in a god-like role in his family, so I thought I should be the Great Provider in my family. Thus, I tried to slap myself out of my grief and into the role I had inherited.

To be honest, I rather enjoyed playing god for a time! I felt extremely responsible, and I was sure my own father, now watching my every move from heaven, was pleased with my performance. I rather suspect my pleasure was like that of the "death of God" theologians, who declared in the sixties that "God is dead and now we must face the future alone." That is heady stuff. When rooted in self-confidence, it makes one feel in control and powerful. I would wake up in the morning, look at the day in front of me, and say, "By George, I'm going to get my act together today, even if I have to kick a few butts in order to do it." It was a real high.

Unfortunately, it was a high from which I had to come down—assuming, that is, that I wanted to face reality. The problem, of course, was that I was not God and therefore my life was a sham. It might have impressed others. I might even have gotten a few people to believe that I was God. But success, when built upon an illusion, is no fun. And, much more importantly, it is destined to fail. In a month or a year or a lifetime. Eventually, your business will go bankrupt or your spouse (who doesn't enjoy living with God) will leave you or your children will rebel or . . . you will die.

I will die. Just as my father did. And then what will happen to my pretense? That, along with a number of other minor frustrations, convinced me that playing god was not the answer to my problem. Too many people would get hurt, for one thing: people that I would push out of my path because they didn't genuflect when I passed; or people who bowed appropriately and, there-fore, lived with the lie themselves. Just as importantly, it did harm to my self—my God-given self. For I wasn't created to be God. I was created to be a man. And the void that I felt deep within my being existed for my good, not my self. That was the lie of Eden. Giving in to the lie leads not to paradise but to exclusion from it. Indeed, it puts one on a perpetual quest for a paradise lost, without the slightest hope of finding satisfaction. And I needed satisfaction. I needed God.

## Conclusion

It is not popular, of course, to admit to needs these days. It's so confining. So unmacho. So dangerous! Far better, we think, is a life of self-sufficiency, where we control our own destinies and use others rather than depend upon them. That's why most of us in the modern world are on a search for a need-free existence; needs confront us with our own insufficiency. That is also why we like to ignore the reality of death; it confronts us with our greatest need of all.

Denying need is not an escape, however, it's a modern tragedy. It's a tragedy, for one thing, because we do need others. We were created to live with one another and to supply one another's needs. That's another reason that grief in loss is both appropriate and inevitable. We are diminished by another's death to the extent that we are involved in each other's lives.[16] The human community requires the contributions of each of its parts. And when the parts get lost or can't play their role, the whole community suffers. It ought to make us cry.

But we also have needs that no human can or ought to fill. And that was the lesson I learned through the death of my father. I was blessed with a dad who was willing to shoulder his responsibility in the human family. He played his part, and he played it well. And I was the beneficiary of his willingness to live as if others needed him. But I took his responsibility for granted and transformed it into something it was not designed to be. In doing that, I was fair neither to him nor to myself. Most of all, I was not being honest with God.

Thus, through the agony of my grief and my forsakenness, I not only shed the pretensions of idolatry, but I also finally came to understand the most important truth of all: The Lord alone is God.

That is a marvelous thing, by the way. It ought to bring us comfort even in the midst of the loss of a loved one. The One who can supply our ultimate needs can never be taken from us. The loss of God is a grief that none of us needs to bear.[17]

# 5

## Knowledge: Loss of God

ıııııııııııııııııııııııııııııııııııııııııııııııııııııııııııııııııııııııııııııııııııııııııııııı

And yet, some of us do bear the loss of God. Indeed, the wisest of us all knew precisely what it meant to bear the loss of God. And the relationship between his wisdom and his sense of loss is not coincidental. Listen to the words of Solomon:

> I, the Teacher, was king over Israel in Jerusalem. I devoted myself to study and to explore by wisdom all that is done under heaven. What a heavy burden God has laid on men! I have seen all the things that are done under the sun; all of them are meaningless, a chasing after the wind. What is twisted cannot be straightened; what is lacking cannot be counted.
>
> I thought to myself, "Look, I have grown and increased in wisdom more than anyone who has ruled over Jerusalem before me; I have experienced much of wisdom and knowledge." Then I applied myself to the understanding of wisdom, and also of madness and folly, but I learned that this, too, is a chasing after the wind. For with much wisdom comes much sorrow; the more knowledge, the more grief (Eccles. 1:12–18).
>
> "Meaningless! Meaningless!" says the Teacher. "Utterly meaningless! Everything is meaningless." (Eccles. 1:2)

## A Perplexing Introduction

I am a professor. Wisdom and knowledge are my stock-in-trade. They are not only the things I seek, but they are the commodities in which I deal. Indeed, unless others want them, I receive no salary. More importantly, I believe they are valuable. So valuable, in fact, that whether or not I got paid, I believe I would continue to pursue them and share them with others. Wisdom and knowledge are, from my perspective, pearls of great worth.

The Bible shares my enthusiasm, fortunately.

> Choose my instruction instead of silver, knowledge rather than choice gold; for wisdom is more precious than rubies, and nothing you desire can compare with her (Prov. 8:10–11).
>
> How much better to get wisdom than gold, to choose understanding rather than silver! . . . Whoever gives heed to instruction prospers, and blessed is he who trusts in the Lord (Prov. 16:16, 20).
>
> He who gets wisdom loves his own soul; he who cherishes understanding prospers (Prov. 19:8).
>
> By wisdom a house is built, and through understanding it is established; through knowledge its rooms are filled with rare and beautiful treasures (Prov. 24:3–4).

These verses are only a few of the many Scripture passages that extol wisdom and knowledge. Obviously, my appreciation for them is not simply a personal idiosyncrasy. Nor is it something I invented to legitimate my wages. The Lord himself values wisdom and knowledge, encourages us to pursue them, and considers them far more attention-worthy than most of the things that typically tap our passions. Those who wish to become students, we can say with confidence, aspire to a noble task.

And yet the same writer who proclaimed the worth of wisdom and knowledge also confessed to their meaninglessness. The same Solomon who encourages God's people to seek wisdom and knowledge also laments that attaining them leads only to sorrow and grief. Without doing any damage to the text, we could say that Solomon not only exhorts us to gain knowledge and wisdom but also warns us that in finding them, we'll discover a painful loss as well.

How can this be true? Why should something so obviously good have such a painful effect? If this paradox were not expressed in the inspired Word of God, we might be tempted to question its veracity. Some are tempted still, but that's not my bent. I find the paradox easy to accept, not only because it's scriptural but also because Solomon's message rings true in my own life.

## The Worth of Knowledge

Without doubt, there is something wonderful about discovering knowledge and wisdom. Learning is a grand adventure. Two things make learning special. First, learning isn't easy; it always takes work. I know of few people who begin the study of a new subject with enthusiasm. That's because the initial process is 90 percent drudgery. For this reason, most of us would rather not even get started. We avoid work, and thus we avoid learning. But the necessity of work is precisely what makes learning so pleasurable once it is discovered.

Think of the pleasures of eating, or of sex, for example. They too require the exertion of energy. But the pleasure in them is apparent right from the start. All I have to do is think about a pizza, and my mouth begins to water. Indeed, the pleasure begins before the activity even gets started.

But learning is rarely like that. Its pleasure comes only after an initial stage of pain and effort. For that reason, however, its pleasure is always a surprise and its result always a fulfillment. A good meal may not live up to its billing, and it usually leaves one feeling a bit bloated. Discovery, however, is never a disappointment. Its enjoyment is always greater than anticipated.

Second, learning is special because its product is enduring. Let's return to food for a moment (a much safer topic than sex). Food is a good thing, certainly, given to us by our Creator for our enjoyment and our sustenance. But it's also temporal. Four hours after I've eaten my last meal, I'm feeling hungry again, and I'm in hot pursuit of more mouth-watering delights.

Learning is not like that, however. Once ingested, it provides pleasure for years and years to come. Though it never fully satisfies (like food), the satisfaction it brings endures and makes possible the acquisition of new kinds of knowledge.

All of this I know from experience. I've tried both ignorance and knowledge, and I can attest to the superiority of the latter. And yet, from experience I know something else as well. Despite the joy that learning brings, the knowledge that comes with it is a double-edged sword. With one edge, error is slain and understanding gains a great victory. But with the other edge, dilemmas and perplexities of unimagined proportion are revealed.

## The Triumph of Knowledge

At some risk, I want to introduce such a double-edged sword in my own thinking. It's a risk, not only because it exposes the limits of my own imagination, but because in pursuing this topic, I may be introducing a problem the reader isn't prepared to handle. Nevertheless, to talk in abstraction is to say nothing at all. This subject, just like the others, deserves to be illustrated. And honesty precludes the use of anything but a realistic example. This double-edged sword has an academic title, but I think it is better understood in context.[1]

Let's say you have become the pastor of a struggling congregation. The church has a membership of over two hundred, but only about a hundred people show up on any given Sunday morning. It has a reputation as a dull church, and most people who attend seem to fit that description perfectly.

You come into the church, however, with a vision for evangelism and church renewal. So the first Sunday you begin preaching from the Book of Romans, laying a theological foundation for Christian outreach. After six months in Romans, you spend another six months in the Book of Acts in an attempt to give your congregation a glimpse of what is possible when the spirit of God moves among his people. Your sermons are well received, but the effect is less than earth shaking. Few new converts. Little church growth. And the church seems as dull as ever.

You become discouraged. You plunge into books, hoping that they will either cure your mood or provide you with a solution to your problem. The book you choose this time happens to be on the sociology of

religion. You pick it because you once enjoyed an
undergraduate course on that topic and because you
vaguely remember discussions relating to the frustrations of the modern pastorate. Maybe you will gain some
insight there, you think.

The book is a surprise, however. What stands out is
not the chapter on the role of the pastor, but the
description of modern men and women: lonely, lacking
in durable relationships, bombarded by choices they
can't handle, they are dissatisfied with yesterday's answers, panting after tomorrow's opportunities, insecure
in their status, and unable to affirm the truth of anything
beyond their own self-interests.[2] These, you learn, are
the inhabitants of the "secular society."[3] What really
strikes you, however, is how this same secular society
seems to spin out one new religious movement after
another. How is it, you ask yourself, that hundreds of
bizarre religious "cults" (as you call them) can flourish in
such a secular environment?[4]

And then it hits you. The cult flourishes not in spite of
the secular society but because of it. The cult offers
precisely those things that people need but that modern
society is unable to provide. To those who are lonely and
without dependable relationships, the cult provides a
strong sense of community, dripping with acceptance
and support. To those confused by the plethora of
modern choices and dilemmas, the cult provides simple
answers to every question and a charismatic leader to
explain all truth. And to those who are unsure of
themselves or their place in life, the cult offers absolute
security; "place yourself in our hands," says the cult,
"and you need never worry about your future again."[5]

Though the facts themselves are disturbing, your new-found insight about the facts is exciting. It's one of those "aha!" experiences, when you're suddenly able to make sense out of previously nonsensical material. But your excitement doesn't stop there. Remember, you're the pastor of a struggling church. And you begin to wonder how your insight relates to the struggles of your church. After all, your congregation is full of modern people. Are they dealing with the same insecurities and dilemmas other modern people contend with? If so, what does that tell you about your church and your role as a pastor?

It isn't long before you realize why your congregation isn't responding to your pastoral leadership. You've been giving them theological options in a world of ideological options, and they're looking for truth. You're giving them a one-hour program every Sunday morning in a world of one-hour programs, and they need a genuine community. You're making them feel anxious about their Christian witness in a world of high anxiety, and they're on a desperate search for security. In other words, you're competing with the world. And losing. And in the process, you're meeting none of their most basic needs.

You determine to change. For the sake of space, we won't describe how you manage the task, but we'll assume you put together a program that takes into account your sociological insight about the nature of modern society. You take great care to develop an approach that is consistent with your understanding of Scripture. But the guiding light behind your program is the notion that the church must meet the needs of the modern parishioner. As a result, you emphasize simple truths, the importance of the church "family," interpersonal accountability among community members, and the security that comes from being a part of such a community. While you're careful not to incorporate the manipulative tendencies of the modern cult, you have nevertheless learned from them, borrowing some of their clichés, their methods, and not a few of their values.[6]

Well, the results are phenomenal. Within a short time, your church is growing vigorously, and your congregation exhibits a vibrancy that visitors notice and other pastors envy. Soon people begin to ask you to speak at nearby colleges and universities, and denominational leaders call you up to ask for your advice and assistance. As you share your wisdom about church renewal with other pastors, they encourage you to lecture and possibly write a book about your experiences. Eventually, you take them up on their advice, putting together a treatise that even your critics describe as "the modern manual on church renewal." In a short amount of time, then, you have taken a small insight (knowledge), applied it to a particular problem (wisdom), and gained fame and success as a result. And you have never felt more fulfilled in all your life.

### Forsakenness of Knowledge

But then, a couple of things happen, clouding the picture a bit. The first is that other pastors begin using your approach to church renewal, and, lo and behold, they have the same success as you. This, of course, is what your book says will happen, so you ought to be thrilled by the news. But you are thrilled only in public. In private, the idea that others could be employing your methods—and succeeding—is terribly troubling.

Second, over time, even your own church's success begins to bother you a bit. You're not sure why, but sometimes when one of your staff members runs into your office to report some grand church statistic, you want to throw him out on his ear. It's almost as if you wished the program were not working so well. The problem isn't that you're bored with your work; the task itself is still very exciting. It's the meaning of your success that really is starting to get you down.

The reason for your dispirited state, however, doesn't fully surface until you finally visit one of your church clones. Sitting there in the pew of another church, watching the same program generate the same happy faces, you begin to wonder: What do all these happy faces mean? When you first encountered them in your church, they seemed so wonderful. So meaningful. So authentic. But now that you've seen them a thousand times before—at home, and now instantly recreated in another church—the wonder seems to have vanished. How can duplicates be authentic? How can assembly-line renewal have any ultimate significance? What great value is there, after all, in a religious cookie cutter?

A sociologist would describe your condition as *anomie*. It occurs whenever something loses its ultimate significance.[7] In this case, it has occurred because a matter that was once personally meaningful to you, church renewal, now seems to be nothing more than a consequence of social circumstances. What you have discovered, in other words, is that the spiritual vibrancy of a church is relative to its social setting. The positive side of this discovery is that through it you were able to make your church come alive. That's why you went from preaching about church renewal to setting up the conditions that would bring it into being. The negative side, however, is that, once you really understood its implications, the significance of the renewal was totally lost for you.

To state it simply, you went into the church hoping the Lord would bring renewal. Now that renewal has been achieved, however, it seems as if the Lord had nothing to do with it. Renewal, in fact, seems altogether relative to social conditions. If one designs the right environment, the people seem to respond. What you've done is to create the conditions for renewal. You have become something of a god, in other words, and in the process you've lost the God you originally intended to serve. Thus, what you accomplished has lost its meaning, and at the pinnacle of success, you have no One above you to share it with.

From a Christian perspective, of course, we have been witness to a terrible theological blunder. The pastor assumed that since he had established the conditions that brought about renewal, God had nothing to do with it.[8] That is bad theology. The Bible repeatedly shows us that God works through our actions to bring about his plans. It was neither the pastor nor his social engineering that brought about renewal. If the renewal was the genuine article, it was God's Spirit that brought it into being.[9]

Unfortunately, that bit of theology may not eliminate the feeling of God's absence. It's so much easier, after all, to believe God is at work when something happens for which there can be no human accounting. Like parting the Red Sea, for example. Or water that suddenly becomes wine. Or Lazarus walking out of his grave. There is no better evidence of God's involvement in human existence than miracles.

In contrast, when something results from our own

knowledge or wisdom, it appears to be a function of our efforts, not his. That's why increased knowledge often leads to greater self-reliance. As we gain knowledge about something, we assume a certain mastery over it, a sense of control. Self-reliance, in turn, tends to bolster our ego; in biblical language, self-reliance often fosters pride. The haughty attitude that one senses among college faculty, then, is no accident. It is the natural outgrowth of the knowledge industry of which they are a part.

But "pride goeth before a fall" and, in this case, the fall is rather profound. With intellectual pride also comes a loss of meaning. You see, in spite of how much we enjoy mastering our own fate and being in control of our world, the world itself is much more meaningful when we see God's hand at work within it. When we lose the sense of his presence, we lose more than a theological concept. We lose the meaning behind our own existence as well.

The pastor in our example found this out the hard way. He didn't begin his ministry with the intention of losing touch with God or losing his sense of meaning. Indeed, he was giving his all for the Lord. That's why he went into the pastorate in the first place, and that's why he wanted his church to grow. But something happened along the way. Maybe it occurred when he began thinking of the church as *his* church; maybe it happened when he linked the lack of vibrancy in the church to *his* own failure. However it took place, it led him into a search inspired not by a love of learning but by a desire to master his environment.

That motive didn't make the learning any less enjoyable, of course. He still thrilled at his discoveries and rejoiced in their application. But it did enable him to assume that the learning itself was purely his accomplishment. When he successfully applied *his* wisdom to *his* church, therefore, that too was *his* accomplishment.

God had been removed from the scene, not by a conscious decision, but by an assumption about the source of knowledge. With every new discovery, the size of God diminished. With every bit of success, the pastor gained evidence of his control and God's absence. Thus, with increased knowledge, his sense of cosmic loneliness increased as well. And the reason for his calling to the pastorate totally vanished. His knowledge, along with his life, had lost its purpose. In the words of Solomon, it now seemed meaningless, a chasing after the wind.

Some would argue, of course, that he was only losing a fantasy, and thus, the loss is insignificant. I tend to think that argument is contradicted by the lives of those who assume it. It's not hard to argue that God doesn't exist, of course. That has been attempted from time immemorial. What is far more difficult, however, is to live consistently as if he doesn't exist. Indeed, aside from those who commit suicide over the matter, I see very little evidence it can be done. Everyday human expressions—from laughter, to righteous indignation, to play—all seem to point to the need for some Greater Significance.[10]

For good reason, I believe. We are not alone. We were created. We are, in the deepest possible sense, dependent, not independent. Thus, we need our Creator. One of the things that we need him for is to give purpose and meaning to our lives. We crave meaning in our lives not because we need a fantasy to sustain us but because Reality has created us with such a need.

## The God of Knowledge

Thus, we come to what may seem a rather unsettling conclusion. The God who created us is the One who gives meaning to our lives. For that reason, we are able to learn about his world—to gain knowledge and wisdom about our own condition. With that knowledge, however, often comes self-reliance and pride—the temptation to supplant God with ourselves. When we do that, however, we are suddenly left with only ourselves. Alone. And without our source of meaning. And thus we lose the One who enabled us to learn in the first place.

Why should this be? Isn't there something a bit unfair in all of this? Why shouldn't knowledge lead only to a deeper understanding of God? Why would God also allow it to bring us to the point of meaninglessness and despair?

I don't know. That is the first thing that should be said. With these questions, we are speculating into the mind of God. And that, to say the least, is a dangerous preoccupation.[11]

I will offer this judgment, however. In "knowing" we are engaging in one of the most profoundly God-like activities imaginable. It's not the only such activity, certainly, but it's without a doubt one of the most remarkable. On the one hand, that's why gaining knowledge and wisdom is so exciting and worthwhile. On the other, that's why it gives us such a sense of mastery and control. For that reason, knowledge and wisdom offer us not only the possibility of great joy but also the most tempting opportunity to deny God. To challenge him. To play at being god ourselves.

We are not God, however, and thus every attempt at

usurping his position must ultimately fail. Knowledge, too, must fail when it plays the role of the Almighty. Wisdom, as well, must be revealed as an imposter. Thus, at precisely the point that knowledge brings us to the conclusion that we control our own destiny, it inevitably collapses into meaninglessness. The moment we climb to the top of Mount Olympus, we fall to the depths of despair. The minute we think we understand it all, we realize that we can't even understand ourselves. It's as if the knowledge that bolsters our ego is destined, inevitably, to laugh in our face.

But why should it be otherwise? Why, after all, should a pretender be allowed to remain on the throne? The real puzzle, I would contend, is not why God allows knowledge to lead us into despair. That, if the despair points us back to him, is an act of grace, a forsakenness redeemed. The more unanswerable question is why the Source of our wisdom is willing—for even a day—to put up with our wise pretensions.

### Conclusion

The Lord remains a mystery. But he doesn't leave us without understanding. Indeed, he gives us knowledge and wisdom far beyond what we deserve or merit. With that understanding, however, comes this simple stipulation: Knowledge must be connected to its source in order to remain meaningful. The minute our thinking leads us to our own self-aggrandizement, it leads us to our doom as well. God has woven it into the fabric of his creation. The Author of wisdom can't be excluded from its execution.

That is no small insight, by the way. We live in an age

## The Subject: God ordains certain men to hell on purpose

Isaiah 64:8 - *O Lord, thou art our Father; we are the clay; and thou our potter; and we all are the <u>work</u> of thy hand.*

**work** - Hebrew: Maaseh-an action (good or bad); product; transaction; business

Romans 9:20-23 - *Who art thou that repliest against God? Shall the thing formed say to him that formed it, why hast thou made me thus? Hath not the potter the power over the clay of the same lump, to make one vessel unto honour and another unto dishonour -- What if God willing to show his wrath, and to make his power known, endured with much long suffering the vessels of wrath <u>fitted</u> to destruction: And that he might make known the riches of his glory on the vessels of mercy, which he hath afore prepared unto glory.*

**fitted** - Greek: katartizo - to complete thoroughly; fit; frame; arrange; prepare. Thayer says this word speaks of men whose souls God has so constituted that they cannot escape destruction; <u>their mind is fixed that they frame themselves.</u>

Men get angry to think that we serve a God that can do as it pleases him. They actually think that an almighty God thinks the way they think and that he could not possibly form-fit a vessel to hell merely to show his wrath and power. Paul said he does. Men have difficulty perceiving a God that predestinates men (Rom. 8:29) on whom he desires to show his grace (unmerited favor) and mercy, that he may shower them throughout eternity with the riches of his glory. We like to believe that we must give him permission; if he is to operate in our hearts and minds. The Lord said, "My thoughts are not your thoughts, neither are your ways my ways. As the heavens are higher than the earth, so are my ways higher than your ways and my thoughts than your thoughts (Isaiah 55:8,9)". Our God is in the heavens: he hath done whatsoever he hath pleased (Psalms 115:3). He doeth whatsoever pleaseth him (Eccl 8:3). Thou, O Lord hast done as it pleased thee (Jonah 1:14). Whatsoever the Lord pleased, that did he in heaven, and earth, and in the seas, and in all deep places (Psalms 135:6). He does all his pleasure (Isa. 46:10; Isa. 44:24-28; Eph. 1:5,9; Philippians 2:13). It is Jesus that holds the keys to death and hell (Rev. 1:18), not Satan. God will intentionally cast these evil vessels of wrath into hell and lock them up for eternity because it is not his pleasure to draw them to him (John 6:44). This doctrine angers men, though it is taught throughout the pages of God's Holy Book. Men do not have a Biblical view of the living God when they think he is not in control of all things including the minds and hearts of all men. God is not only love to the vessels of mercy, but he is a consuming fire (Deut 4:24) upon the vessels of wrath fitted to destruction. We do not serve a God who is Superman that can only shake mountains, implode blackholes, and explode quasars. The God of the universe can harden and soften the hearts of men at will (Rom 9:18; Ezek. 36:26). He giveth not account of any of his matters (Job 33:13).

## GRACE AND TRUTH MINISTRIES

P.O. Box 1109 Hendersonville, TN 37077
Jim Brown - Bible Teacher • 824-8502

Radio Broadcast – Sat. Morn. 8am 1300 AM Dial WNQM
TV -- Mon. & Sat 10pm, Wed. & Fri. 12am Channel 176;
Tues. & Thurs. 5pm Channel 3; Thurs. 11am Channel 49

Join us for fellowship at 394 West Main Street on
Sunday Mornings @ 11:00am, Sunday Evenings @ 7:00pm,
Wednesday Evenings @ 7:00pm
Or
Watch us live via U-Stream on the web at
www.graceandtruth.net

when most learned people believe exactly the opposite. Modern science is rooted in the notion that good science must be disconnected from beliefs, for example, and humanities scholars seem convinced that critical thought necessitates rejecting Ultimate Authority. In such an environment, it may take the loss of God to confront us with the limits of our own understanding and the utter futility of knowledge separated from its Creator. In the midst of such loss, some will perish in the waves of nihilism and meaninglessness. But for those with ears to hear, the ageless truth of Scripture will reassert itself with pristine simplicity: "The fear of the Lord is the beginning of wisdom" (Ps. 111:10). And knowledge born out of forsakenness will become, at last, a knowledge redeemed.

# REDEEMING VALUES OF FORSAKENNESS

IIIIIIIIIIIIIIIIIIIIIIIIIIIIIIIIIIIIIIIIIIIIIIIIIIIIIIIIIIIIIIIIIIIIIIIIIIIIIIIIIIIIIIIIIIIIIIIIIIIIIII

It's time to turn our attention to something that has been implicit in these discussions but deserves more frank discussion. Forsakenness is something we feel not only because of circumstances around us but also because of values we hold deep within us. These values both color our interpretation of events and influence the way we behave toward one another. For both reasons, some of these values can produce a sense of forsakenness.

In chapter 6, for example, I will argue that the modern notion of *responsibility* is based on values that are not only unbiblical but also unhealthy because they can lead to forsakenness. These values, which we have absorbed from our society, give us false expectations about human behavior. As we will see, such expectations make it quite likely that we will one day feel abandoned by others.

In chapter 7, however, we turn from the effect of values on expectations to their effect on behavior. Here I will attempt to show how some of the values we get from our society actually encourage us to forsake one another. The focus of this chapter will be the value of *independence*, a value which has a long and noble heritage in our society but which, in the modern era, has come to be used in very ignoble ways.

Nevertheless, social experiences, like personal experiences, can be redeemed. And we will look for the redemptive possibilities in our society as well.

# 6

## *Responsibility: Loss of Control*

||||||||||||||||||||||||||||||||||||||||||||||||||||||||||||||||||||||||||||||||||||||||||||||||||||||||||||||||||||||||||||||||||||||

*The most important thought I ever had was that of my individual responsibility to God.*

Daniel Webster

You've heard the story before. A mother is in agony over her son's behavior at school. At the age of fourteen, he has suddenly lost all interest in his studies and has abandoned his love of athletics. His teachers say he's not disruptive in class, but he isn't involved either. He just sits there, waiting for the day to end so he can enjoy the company of his peers. It's a new company, and it seems to be the only thing he finds worthwhile in life.

His mother can't understand it. Aside from her husband, her son is the most important person in her life. He was, in the best sense of the word, a wanted child. For the first ten years of their marriage, the couple was childless. After many prayers and almost as many doctors' fees, they finally conceived their one and only child. The boy was brought up with Christian values, abundant love, and much care. For the first thirteen years of his life, that environment seemed to produce a diligent, all-American boy. Now, a year later, it seems to have been all for naught.

## A Question of Responsibility

"How can this have happened?" the mother asks herself. It certainly wasn't the original script. She had always assumed the boy would grow up to be like his father: successful in school, business, and church. But now it appears he'll turn out more like his Uncle Joe, her brother, who never finished high school but has never in his life refused to finish a glass of beer. As she reflects on her dreams for her son and contrasts them with the present reality, she is gripped with two overwhelming feelings. The first is fear. The second is a deep sense of having been forsaken.

The fear relates primarily to the future. She's afraid of what will become of her son, of course, but she is also concerned about herself. The former fear is the one she's willing to talk about, but her fear for herself is the more difficult to deal with. She doesn't think anyone would understand it, for one thing, and besides, it sounds too selfish. You see, she has always thought of herself as a good mother. Others have told her that, complimenting her for her son's good behavior, and she had come to believe it. Part of her identity, then, comes from being a "good mother." If her son goes off the deep end now, she'll not only lose her son, but she'll also lose an important part of her self. Thus, the son's situation represents to her a tragedy as well as a deep, unspeakable embarrassment.

Both fears are related to her sense of forsakenness. With the fear came the realization that things were increasingly getting out of control. Formerly, through responsible parenting, she had thought that she was carving out a respectable life, both for herself and her son. Now with her son's changed behavior, that image is crumbling. It's as if she has molded a sculpture for years, only to awake one morning and discover that her creation has been totally transformed. What has happened? How could it have happened?

The haunting thing, however, was that—now that the transformation had taken place—there seemed so little she could do about it. The creation was still in the workshop, but it suddenly refused to be molded. In other words, although the problem was within her domain of responsibility, it was impervious to her will. The world said that she was responsible for her son. But the reality was that nothing she did—none of the listening, talking, arguing, grounding, etc.—made any difference in his behavior.

His life, and hers, were falling apart. And she could do nothing about it. She felt a deep sense of loss and despair. She felt forsaken.

### Responsibility Reconsidered

What the mother was feeling was accountability without control. It's not supposed to happen in our world. We hold two ideas to be sacrosanct: we're in control of our own lives, and we can choose our own responsibilities. If we follow these two ideas religiously, so the story goes, accountability without control need not exist. Unfortunately, those ideas are either wrong, impossible, or both.

It's sometimes a bit disconcerting to learn that most people throughout human history didn't choose their responsibilities, they inherited them. Before the Industrial Revolution, positions of honor and responsibility were given out at birth. Men became kings not as the result of a lifetime of political maneuvering, electioneering, and campaigning but by virtue of their birth into a royal family. The responsibilities of parenting and marriage were also "givens," since many marriages were prearranged and since most children just "happened" nine months later. These were not positions a person achieved; they were responsibilities a person acquired by virtue of birth.[1]

To us, such an arrangement seems fundamentally flawed. People ought never to be forced into responsibilities, we think. They ought to be able to choose them instead. Mothers should be be able to choose to become mothers. Presidents ought to aspire to become presidents. And all of us ought to have the right to take on the roles for which we are best suited. We find inherited responsibilities neither attractive nor especially fair.

And yet that is our lot in life, even in the modern world. For while it's true that we moderns can sometimes select from a wide array of roles and positions, we have little choice about responsibility itself. It comes with the package. If we want to be human, we must assume responsibility.

Think of an ant. When it hatches, it joins a society of other ants. On the surface, it's a society much like our own. As we peer in on the community, we see creatures moving in numerous directions, accomplishing a wide variety of tasks. Some are building new homes. Others are cleaning and maintaining established residences. Many are searching for additional food supplies (in my cupboard!), and many more are tapping known resources (my garbage can), bringing home the bacon to the main camp.

Now think of a human baby. It too is born into a community of creatures whose behavior is organized around the need for food, shelter, and survival. But though these two communities look similar, there is one fundamental difference. When the ant breaks into its world, it begins immediately to accomplish the tasks for which it was designed. It doesn't require discipline, education, or affection to play its part. It needs only to survive. And if it survives (a big *if* in my cupboard), it will do precisely what its Creator intended.

When we were born, however, what did we do? Well, we spit and sucked and pooped, but not a whole lot more. Not only were we physically incapable of building homes and securing our own food supply, we were totally lacking the wherewithal to accomplish such tasks. In other words, the problem is not merely anatomical. The problem is conditional. To become farmers and engineers, we'll have to *learn* our trade. We'll have to go through many years learning social, linguistic, and technical skills. And, even then, there's no guarantee we'll succeed.[2]

Human communities, then, are not simply "doing" communities, they are "learning" communities. They exist only because their members are able to teach their offspring how to live and because their offspring are able to comprehend and act on the basis of what they have learned. To put it in the language of this chapter, human communities thrive only to the extent that their inhabitants are responsible—willing and able to respond to the instruction of others.[3]

What this means, of course, is that responsibility is a necessary ingredient in human affairs. Though it's not absolutely obligatory (humans can choose not to survive, after all), responsibility is required of those who wish to live.[4] Human life entails responsibility. This is as true of those living in the midst of modernity as anywhere else. We moderns may have much more discretion about how we will be responsible, but we can't opt out of responsibility altogether. It's thrust upon us by the human condition.

## Modern Expectations of Responsibility

The mother in our story illustrates the point. Because she's a modern mother, she was given the privilege of choosing her own responsibilities. She chose to marry, for example. Her parents didn't require marital status of her, and they certainly didn't pre-select her spouse. Though she may have felt a great deal of social pressure to marry, she was under no obligation to do so.

She chose, as well, to have a child. In her case, that was a choice not easily brought to completion. For a number of reasons, she had difficulty carrying a baby full term. Thus, it was ten years before she and her husband finally saw the fruit of their decision to have a child. This waiting period, however, served only to strengthen modern values. Not too many years ago, a woman in her situation would have simply resigned herself to child-lessness. But not this mother. She read books by the dozens and went to medical clinics by the score. In other words, she *took control* of her life. And through will power, money, and a cooperative husband, she finally was able to have the baby she so desperately wanted.

At midlife, then, she not only had imbibed modern values, but she also had put them into practice. And it had paid off. She had chosen her own responsibilities, managed them with confidence, and was now enjoying the product of those values. And her experiences lived up to her expectations: she had an intelligent, well-mannered, good-looking son—an odds-on favorite to become a successful, modern man.

But children aren't simply the product of a modern equation. They're a gift from God. And God's gifts are almost always surprise packages. The mother learned that lesson when her son got into high school. Suddenly her chosen responsibility was acting irresponsibly, and her once-controlled life seemed quite out of control.

You may wonder why she was surprised by her son's behavior. That's a good question. After all, I began describing her story with the words, "You've heard the story before." And we have. Her story isn't unique. Sons and daughters get out of control, despite their parents' best intentions. So why did this mother not expect it to happen to her?

It's important to note that the mother's story is familiar not only because of her son's behavior, but also because of *her response.* Her surprise, fear, and loneliness are also a routine part of the story. The question, then, is not how can she be surprised by her son's behavior but *how can this scenario be repeated in thousands of homes and in each case come as a shock to the people involved?* In other words, how can I watch two or three neighbors go through this experience and then be surprised when it happens to me?

Expectations, it turns out, are the result not only of experience but also of beliefs and values.[5] And in spite of the fact that human life entails responsibility; in spite of the fact that many of those responsibilities are not of our own choosing; in spite of the fact that much in our life is out of our control; in spite of all these experiences with reality, we moderns choose to ignore them. We acknowledge them when they happen to others, but we don't expect them to happen to us.

What we assume, instead, are "happiness values." Happiness values put the self at center stage and suppose that life ought to be designed around its wishes. Happiness values must not be confused with the desire to be happy. All of us want to live a fulfilling life. Instead, happiness values transform a basic desire into a fundamental value and right. Thus, happiness isn't simply a hope for us; it's an everyday objective and an ongoing expectation. We live our lives for the purpose of being happy, and we assume the right to attain a good measure of happiness on a daily basis.[6]

Happiness *values*, however, fly in the face of responsibility *realities*. They operate in two different realms. The *value* tells us that the burdens of life can be effectively managed, that they are mere inconveniences in our march toward successful living. The *reality* is that burdens are the stuff of life. We may find joy through them, or in spite of them, but we will not find it by controlling or avoiding them. But the value inhibits our recognition of the reality. That's why every unwanted responsibility seems like such a shame to us. And that's why the mother in our story was so surprised by her son's behavior.

And that's why she felt forsaken. You see, because she presumed the ability to shape her son's destiny (as well as her own), she assumed a power she didn't really possess. When reality struck, she not only found out her assumption was false, but she also had no support. She didn't expect others to take responsibility for her son, and no one assumed that responsibility. When her parenting failed to produce the desired results, therefore, she felt like a failure—not only in her own eyes but also in the eyes of others. There were no "others" to take partial responsibility for her son's condition, and there were no "others" to offer support in her time of need. She was alone with her problem. A problem she thought she shouldn't have. A problem she thought *others* thought she shouldn't have. And a problem she thought resulted from her own incompetence at living the "good life." This mother was left holding the bag. Alone. And her world couldn't care less.

**Habits of the Heart**

It's easy, of course, to critique the mother's thinking. We conclude: first, she shouldn't have assumed the ability to shape her son's future; second, she should've known that "others" were partly responsible for shaping his life (where was her husband in all of this, anyway?); and third, she should've looked for, and received, support from these "others" in her time of need. Therefore she has no real reason for feeling forsaken.

Ah, what a wondrous thing, the modern mind! Able to critique at a moment's notice. But unable to change a heart in a lifetime of trying.

The problem, remember, is not simply a cognitive one. The mother didn't reach her conclusions by way of a carefully crafted argument. Her thinking, rather, emanated from the heart—a witches' brew of values, feelings, and needs. From that cauldron come the thoughts and actions of everyday life. That's why we readily can analyze our lives but rarely can make changes based on such analyses. It's only when a change of mind is coupled with a change of heart that a changed life results.

And are we any different? Though we may know we don't determine our children's lives, we believe and act as if we do. Though we realize that others have considerable influence on our children, our feelings reveal a very different set of assumptions. One question makes clear what we really believe about such matters: How do we feel when a child goes astray? Or succeeds? What we should feel is grief in the one case and joy in the other. What we often feel, instead, is guilt and pride.

Parental guilt, of course, is sometimes deserved. Parents can act out of pure self-interest and consciously make decisions they know are bad for their children. Guilt in such cases is certainly appropriate.

But much modern guilt is not of this kind. Rather, it results from the parents' suspicion that they may have used the wrong child-rearing technique—that they used Freud when they should have used Skinner, and now their children are paying the price. In other words, the assumption is that if the parents had designed a better environment, then the child wouldn't have gone off the deep end. Parental guilt in such cases, results not from the recognition of sin but because the parents know they have violated a modern assumption. And the judge isn't God, it's the concept of determinism.[7]

Parental pride, on the other hand, is never deserved. When Pete scores well on his math test or Rachel cracks a home run, the response should be joy, not pride. Certainly a loving parent ought to rejoice in a child's accomplishment. But it's the *child's* accomplishment, not the parent's, regardless of the parent's impact on the child's life. At best, a parent can create an atmosphere where good choices and talents can be exercised.[8] But such upbringing will not necessarily result in good behavior, high math scores, or athletic prowess. That's because the choices and talents remain the child's, not the parent's. No parent can take credit for a child's behavior.[9]

Nevertheless, modern parents are filled with both pride and guilt. We strut when our children make the honor roll. We hide our heads when they strike out with the bases loaded. We soar when they give an impeccable Mozart performance on the piano. And we tremble and shake at the thought that they might one day go off the deep end.

And when they do, we wonder what went wrong. Where did we fail? What will others think of us? How can we ever face the world again? In brief, we blame ourselves for our children's choices, and in our embarrassment, probably cut ourselves off from others at the moment we need them the most.

## Modern Responsibility

At the core of such experiences lie two questions: who are we as human beings, and what does it mean to be responsible? If we accept the modern answer to those questions, then our feelings of forsakenness are either justified, meaningless, or both. If we pursue a Christian response, however, we have the possibility of a different outcome, as we'll see in the next section.

In a sense, there is no single modern answer to these questions; one of the hallmarks of modernity, after all, is its ability to generate a multiplicity of debates around every question. Thus, it sometimes leaves us with the impression that moderns aren't in agreement on anything. But if we move from the level of debate to practice, a very different picture emerges.

Our language betrays us. When we discuss human beings today, we primarily use the language of cause and effect. Humans, it turns out, can be on either side of this equation. Thus, on the one hand, we talk about managing people, shaping children, and designing lives. This suggests that humans have great power over others. When looking at the result of such activity, however, we discuss the human being as a product, an outcome, or an effect. This, of course, assumes impotence. Superficially, then, we seem to vacillate between two extremely different conceptions of humanity.

In truth, however, only a single metaphor is being employed and its meaning is not a bit ambiguous. Think of a set of dominoes lined up in a row, each domino standing on its end. When the first domino is toppled, it knocks over the second, which in turn topples the third, and so on. Now, we might ask, is the third domino powerful? Well, if you were the fourth domino you would say "yes," but if you were the second, you would say "no." However, if you were watching the process from the outside, you would say the question is meaningless. The domino is simply one part of a chain reaction. Similarly, when we talk about human beings in causal terms, we appear to be saying that some are extremely influential, while others are not; but in truth we are saying that it's a meaningless question. Every human being is simply one part of an extended sequence of events.

In such an arrangement, of course, "responsibility" is a nonsequitur. Whatever else a domino may be, it certainly is not able to respond. It's incapable of doing anything other than falling after it has been fallen upon. Nevertheless, we do use the term "responsibility" in the modern world, so what do we mean by it? It's my impression that most moderns aren't quite sure. But in general, the term is used to describe the actions of the toppling domino (parent) rather than the one being toppled (child). Since the toppling domino is viewed as the cause of the toppled domino's behavior, responsibility becomes equated with "all powerful," and the responsible person is considered the party of blame.

And that is precisely the position of modern, responsible parents. If they take their responsibility seriously, they are likely to consider themselves the cause of their child's behavior. This leaves them with much pride when things go well but much guilt and loneliness when their child strays. The only way out of this predicament is to see through the whole charade, assume other dominoes are the cause of the predicament, and abandon the responsibility game all together. While this option does free us of the burden of modern responsibility, it has the unpleasant side effect of making our lives utterly meaningless in the process.[10]

## Biblical Responsibility

It's perhaps evidence of how modern we Christians have become that we are one of the primary victims of this form of forsakenness. On the one hand, we're Christian enough in our thinking to know that the "meaningless option" isn't available to us. On the other hand, we aren't biblical enough to recognize that the modern notion of "responsibility" is an imposter. This often leaves us precisely in the modern responsibility predicament, feeling pride when we ought to be rejoicing and feeling solitary guilt when we ought to be grieving in the company of the committed.

The biblical image of the human being, of course, is nothing like a domino. Created in the image of God, the human being is at once a social being influencing others, yet responsible before God for his or her own behavior. We must maintain three biblical truths.

First, we have great influence upon the lives of others. This means we don't live in a vacuum. We live with others, by God's own design, and we fulfill deep needs within one another. Not only do we rely upon others for many of our material needs (food, shelter, etc.), but we need one another for emotional and spiritual support as well. It's through others that we receive love and affection, and it's through the testimony of others that we learn about the God of the universe. Nothing testifies to the importance of human influence more than the fact that God relies upon human beings to declare his glory. All of this suggests that our influence on one another's lives is profound.

Second, we choose how to be influenced by others. We have choices. These choices are highly constrained by who we are, what we are, and where we live. A president's choices are far different from a ghetto dweller's, for example. But in each case, choice always exists. At the very least, one can choose whether or not to go along with a particular kind of influence.

Third, we are accountable to God, both for the ways we influence and for the ways we choose. We are to love others and not tempt them to do evil. Both love and temptation are types of influences, and God expects us to do one and not the other. But when we are tempted, we are to run from evil, not give in to it. When we are confronted by hatred, we are to love, not hate in return. Thus, God doesn't expect us to go along with every influence that comes our way. We are to seek out some influences (the counsel of the godly) and turn away from others (the counsel of the wicked), and we will be held accountable by God for the influences that hold sway in our lives.

Now, all of this is little more than basic Sunday-school material, but it has one very significant implication: We are responsible *to* God and *to* other people, but we are only responsible *for* ourselves. In relation to others, then, we are responsible to them, but not for their behavior. We are responsible to love and feed them, for example, but we are not responsible for what they do with our love and food.

The reason is twofold. One, we are not God. To assume responsibility for someone else's behavior, however, is to assume omnipotence. That is both wrong and dangerous. Secondly, to assume responsibility for someone else's behavior is to deny that person's humanity. That is because such an attitude denies that God gave that person the possibility of exercising choice. When we take responsibility for another's behavior, we demean both God and those whom he has created.

Thus, we come to a conclusion that is biblical but very difficult for modern Christians to accept: Parents are responsible to their children—and will be held accountable by God to properly exercise that responsibility—but they are not responsible for their children's behavior. Not in an ultimate sense, certainly. But as their children mature, not in a practical sense either. Children are responsible for themselves.

Now, please don't misunderstand this statement. Clearly, parents are responsible in the sense that they must teach their children, provide for their needs, and so on. Parents, too, are responsible for monitoring their children's behavior and basing their discipline on performance. A parent who doesn't monitor a child's behavior and respond appropriately is not being responsible either to God or to the child.[11] Nothing here implies that parents ought to be soft disciplinarians, for example. Nevertheless, a parent is not ultimately responsible for the child's behavior. That kind of responsibility belongs to the child alone.

Hard to believe, isn't it? At least, I find it so. But why do I and many other Christians find it so hard to accept an obvious biblical truth? Partly, I think, it's because we've imbibed the spirit of our age. Modernity has taught us that we are responsible for our children's behavior, and we have learned its lessons well. Family specialists, following a deterministic behavioral science, have told us that if we push certain buttons and flip certain switches, our children will behave in certain ways. And, in spite of the fact that it never works out that way, we Christians keep trying because we so desperately want "good children."

But we also find this truth hard to accept because we've come to believe that being responsible for our children's behavior makes us better parents. It not only sounds better, but it makes us seem more caring, more understanding, more of what every parent should aspire to be. But does it? Do you think you will be a better parent if you take responsibility for your child's behavior or if you are responsible to God for how you parent? The first not only will lead to false pride or guilt but it will also encourage you to identify too much with the child's behavior. The object of parenting, after all, is not to raise a first-prize steer. Nor is it to train a pet to bark, roll over on command, or never leave the yard. The object of parenting is to work oneself out of a job; to enable one's children to become responsible for themselves and to their Creator. Responsibility, however, doesn't come to Skinner's rats. Responsibility comes only to those who have freely chosen it.

## Conclusion

The tragedy, of course, is that some people will not choose responsibility. That's a fact of life. And even more tragically, some of those will be our children, our employees, our people. For regardless of how successful we are in living the Christ-life, people over whom we have authority—people to whom we are responsible—will sometimes make irresponsible decisions. Jesus had his Judas. How in the world, then, can we assume that we will escape the irresponsibility of others?

The question is not whether it will happen, but *how we will respond* when it does. Love, it seems to me, dictates at least two responses. First, there ought to be sorrow, and second, there should be responsible action aimed at discouraging future acts of irresponsibility. What there should not be is false guilt or a sense of abandonment.

But there will be both. That is because it's not easy to determine between false guilt and legitimate guilt. Most of us have plenty of reasons to feel guilty about numerous things, giving false guilt more than ample opportunity to masquerade as the real thing. But it's also because we are modern folk, with an all-consuming sense of responsibility for the behavior of those put under our charge. That is why the pulse races when the report card comes home. That is why an inner voice cries "guilty" when it carries a bad report. And that is why we feel oh-so-lonely in the midst of our responsibilities.

For us, the message of this chapter contains good news as well as bad. The bad news is that responsibility is unavoidable. We can't escape it—or the resultant sense of abandonment—by changing spouses or children or any other part of our environment. To be human is to live with responsibilities.

But the good news is that the forsakenness we feel is the result of a false understanding of responsibility. It comes to those who feel responsible for the behavior of others. It does so because, quite often, the behavior of those same others seems out of control. And, to some extent, it is. We can't control the actions of others by feeling responsible for their behavior. We can only live with the effects of a false sense of responsibility.

But there is an alternative. This forsakenness, too, can be redeemed. We can give ourselves to the task of being responsible agents of the Lord God Almighty, rather than playing at being God ourselves. In that case, we will hold ourselves responsible not for the behavior of others but for distributing the love of Christ to all whom he has placed along our way. Thus, our joy will not depend upon the responses of those we love but will flow from the service that we render.

# 7

## *Independence: Rejection by Society*

||||||||||||||||||||||||||||||||||||||||||||||||||||||||||||||||||||||||||||||||||||||||||||||||||||

*A Christian is the most free lord of all,*
*and subject to none;*
*a Christian is the most dutiful servant of all,*
*and subject to everyone.*

Martin Luther

A number of years ago, my son and I were driving to Ipswich to pick up a pizza. Nathaniel was only about five years old at the time, and as children often do, he made an inappropriate comment. Unfortunately, I wasn't in the mood for inappropriate comments. Instead of giving him the simple reprimand he deserved, I lit into him with every argument I could think of. When I concluded my harangue, Nathaniel didn't say a word. He just sat there, looking out the window. Finally, after a considerable interlude, Nathaniel broke the silence.

"You know what, Dad?" he said, with no intention of asking a question. "When I grow up, I think I'm going to live all by myself on top of a mountain."

### The Spirit of Independence

Ah, sweet freedom. Independence. I suppose all of us have heard its call at one time or another. Like my son, we often heard it beckon us as children, when we wanted to be free of limits and lectures. We listened to its voice again as adolescents, when we chafed at parents and parietals. And we hear it call us even as adults, when the burdens of job, church, and home seem too much to bear. "Living alone on a mountain top" is not merely a childhood fantasy. At times, it seems like a good alternative.

The notion of independence is buried deep in our history as well as our psyche. Most of us, in fact, will find that our roots are grounded in the concept. I, for example, come from a long line of Mennonites, a segment of the Anabaptist tradition. From the beginning the Mennonites were a people in search of religious freedom. Because they had "strange" practices and ideas (such as the necessity of adult baptism and the separation of church and state), they were often the objects of persecution and degradation. Fleeing harassment, they found themselves on a perpetual search for freedom, moving to all corners of Europe and America in the process.[1]

But notice something else about my ancestors' experience. Though they were trying to avoid persecution, persecution was not the primary cause of their experience. Indeed, the persecution was actually a reaction to something else. The first cause of the Mennonite experience was the *desire* of these early Anabaptists to practice the Christian faith differently. They had the nerve to assume, in other words, not only that other Christians were practicing their faith wrongly but also that they had the right to go off on their own and practice their faith as they pleased. That's why other Christians persecuted them, and that's why they were forced to move all around God's good earth to practice their beliefs. At the core of the Anabaptist experience, then, is the assumption that one has the right to be independent of the traditions of the past.

In this way, my background is no different from yours. If you are a Protestant, your denomination exists because someone wanted to be independent from the Roman Catholic Church or, more likely, from another Protestant denomination. If you are a Christian (of any stripe), your heritage exists because Jesus' disciples were willing, for the sake of Christ, to break with the traditions of their day.[2] In other words, almost all of us in the Western world trace our ancestry to those who were willing to make a radical departure from the traditions of the past.

## The Modern Spirit

In the last few hundred years, however, the spirit of independence has taken a different turn. Before the eighteenth century, acts of freedom for Jews and Christians were almost always predicated on one objective: To live in obedience to God's will.[3] That is, people were willing to break with the human traditions for the sake of God. In that sense, what motivated them was not a spirit of independence but a desire to live in harmony with their Creator. Independence was not an end in itself but an assumed means to right living before a holy and righteous God.

During the eighteenth and nineteenth centuries, however, two events forever altered our notion of freedom. The first was the Enlightenment, best captured, I think, by the French Revolution.[4] The Enlightenment was an immensely hopeful movement, but its hope was rooted in the human capacity to understand itself and to throw off the oppressions of the past. Thus, in the French Revolution, it was assumed that if traditional powers were deposed (notably, the aristocracy and the church), individual citizens would finally be free to live as nature intended. The revolution, of course, was a dismal failure, but the Enlightenment view of freedom was a grand success. Indeed, from that time on, freedom would be seen not only as an individual right but also as a *goal* to which Western men and women should aspire.

The second pivotal event has also been called a revolution, though it was social and economic in nature, not political. And it was immensely successful. It, of course, is the Industrial Revolution, and it spread rapidly throughout the Western world. This isn't the place to explain either how or why it occurred, but we do need to understand its effects. With the Industrial Revolution came a profound social upheaval, changing dramatically the way most people lived. Agricultural work suddenly vanished, and urban factory jobs sprang up in their place. This caused a tremendous population shift, both from the country to the city and from the Old World to the New. As a result, extended families were split apart, traditional stable communities disappeared, a new middle class gained wealth and prestige, and urban poverty flourished.[5]

Now, the important thing to note is that this social disruption was occurring at precisely the same time the Enlightenment's notion of freedom was catching on. That was no coincidence. "Individual freedom" wasn't an especially attractive idea in the midst of a strong community. Indeed, members of traditional communities often consider individual freedom to be a severe form of punishment. A curse from God. To lose one's community is to lose one's identity. Nothing could be worse.[6]

But when community breaks down, as it did during the Industrial Revolution, people are forced to rethink their view of the world. "If I can't find security in the group (be it family, church, neighborhood, or whatever), where can I find it?" Many people in the new age found their answer in the Enlightenment's optimistic view of the individual. "I'll find my security in myself. I'll shape my world according to my own interests and fight for my right to do so." This was a tremendously powerful idea, and it penetrated the hearts and minds of Western people. It certainly caught the attention of those in the American republic, for example. The right to "life, liberty, and the pursuit of happiness" became a cornerstone idea in the American consciousness.

And its popularity goes unabated today. Indeed, not only do we think of freedom as an important objective but we also have come to define it in increasingly subjective terms. Five hundred years ago, freedom meant the opportunity to live in obedience to God's Word. Two hundred years ago, freedom meant the right to participate in the political process. One hundred years ago, freedom meant the opportunity to move across oceans and mountains to start a new way of life. Fifty years ago, freedom meant "a chicken in every pot, a car in every garage." Today, freedom means anything you want it to mean, from the right of a man to walk out on his responsibilities to the right of a woman to terminate the life of her fetus. Any freedom is justified, as long as it will make us happy.

We find something terribly attractive about this modern notion of freedom. On the one hand, it encourages us to jettison those things that encumber us—those people and communities that inhibit our behavior and keep us from doing what we want. Nobody enjoys enduring senseless restrictions, especially when they get in the way of our own happiness. On the other hand, the modern notion of freedom makes us feel good about not enduring them. After all, isn't freedom a good thing? Isn't it the American way? Don't I have a right to pursue independence? The answer we give to these questions is an unqualified yes. Independence, we believe, is a fundamentally good thing.

## The Spirit of a Forsaken People

And yet, independence clearly leads to forsakenness. Examples fill our newspapers, our movies, our minds. There is the wife who can no longer bear the drudgeries of children and potty training, who leaves town with another man. Or the husband who can no longer bear to be without the woman of his dreams, who leaves the reality of his wife and children behind. Or the pastor who decides that his parish is a pain, and departs for parts unknown. The list is endless, but the story is the same. People searching for nirvana, busting loose from the ties that bind, and leaving in their wake scores of forsaken people.

Not all modern exits are so scandalous, of course. Indeed, some flights of independence are *expected* in our world. A classic example is the young adult who leaves home to strike out on his or her own. The example is classic not only because it happens often but also because we expect it to happen. We've even formalized the event, creating rituals and ceremonies (rites of passage) to guide us through the process. Graduations, college admissions procedures, and marriage ceremonies are just a few of the ways that modern people handle the separation of children from the family. In each case, the parent is encouraged to celebrate the separation, and the child is transferred to a new stage of life.

But it doesn't work. Oh, in a sociological sense, it works, I suppose. It certainly does get Jonathan or Jennifer out the door and into the independent roles society wants them to have. In other words, the rituals accomplish the objective of getting parents and children to do something that by inclination they may not want to do. But at the personal level, the ceremony doesn't work. For when the pomp and circumstance are over, we feel a sickening pain at the bottom of our stomach, a strong feeling that something isn't right with the world. We feel a deep sense of personal loss.

For those who have gone through the experience as parents, none of this will come as a surprise. What might be surprising, however, is that children also feel the pain of separation. The only difference is that the rules of the game permit parents to express their feelings. Children, on the other hand, are supposed to define independence as an ultimate good. For them to confess feelings of loss is not only an admission of immaturity but also a failure to live up to social expectations. Few humans have the strength of character to engage in such honesty. And few have it during late adolescence.

And thus, children leave home like proud peacocks, destined for glory and grandeur. But they arrive like chipmunks, their pouches overflowing with bounty but their eyes nervously looking around for a place to call home. They are not only frightened about the future, but they also are desperately fighting the feeling that something terribly important has just been ripped out of their lives. I know. As a college professor, I get to watch freshmen go through this routine every year. The alienation an entering college student feels is unlike any other routine experience in the modern life cycle.

## Beyond the Classics

And yet this experience *is* routine. Though our ancestors would've thought it barbaric, we've come to expect the young to desert their parents. We know it's going to happen, and thus we can prepare ourselves for it. The problem is that most acts of independence in the modern world aren't like that. Rather, they come like sudden lurches, totally surprising the people who observe them, as well as those left behind.[7]

A friend of mine recently had such a surprise. He'd been a faithful employee of a high-tech company for many years, not only as a hard worker, but also as a significant contributor to the success of the business. He'd put in long hours, traveled extensively, and gained a reputation as a good manager. He'd been rewarded handsomely for his hard work. Over the years he'd risen to one of the premier positions in the company.

Without warning, however, he was fired. He came into the office one day, simply was told by his superior that his services were no longer needed, and was asked to leave. That day. The employer gave no reasons for the action, and he felt no need to explain. But it appears my friend was the victim of a merger. His company had been taken over by another, and as a result, he found himself working for a new boss. His new boss either disliked him or decided that a personnel change would be good for business. Whatever the reason, his boss wanted to be free of him. So, as we euphemistically put it, he was "let go."

My friend's experience is not unique. Such firings are an everyday occurrence in the modern world, and my friend was treated no worse than others. Indeed, he was given a generous severance allowance and the services of an employment agency to help him find another job. His boss probably felt pretty good about how the whole thing was handled—money covers a multitude of sins. And besides, that's business. Nobody promised my friend a job for life. Or even justice. He'd seen others get fired before him and had no reason to expect job security for himself.

Unfortunately, that doesn't make our experience any less surprising. Or painful. It only means that many of us are enduring the same pain, over and over again. It's the pain of rejection. The feeling that I'm not wanted. That I don't belong. And in our world, where one earns one's status in the job market, being fired means losing self-esteem as well. While one person says with pride, "I'm a doctor, judge, or professor," another says in humiliation, "I lost my job."

Such experiences are epidemic in our society, however, not because the business world is ruthless, but because our approach to relationships is ruthless. Arbitrary firings, you see, aren't limited to the world of finance. Nor are they the root of the problem. The problem is—whether in business, family, church, or whatever—we often feel no long-term obligation to one another. Instead, relationships for us are simply a means to personal satisfaction. If they serve the cause, fine. If they don't, we have no qualms about freeing ourselves from them. It's the spirit of independence in its most calculating form. And it hurts. People.

## Why Independence?

Why do we want independence, anyway? Why do we initiate an action that probably will lead others—and possibly ourselves—to despair?[8]

The simple answer is, individual acts of independence are undertaken on behalf of the self. We assume they're good for us. We believe they'll make us happy, bring us pleasure, or free us from frustration. Sometimes we hope they'll help the victim as well (e.g. "I fired him for his own good."). However, most acts of independence are done to free us from costly or offensive relationships.[9]

This doesn't mean that all such acts are wrong, by the way. The battered wife who leaves her husband is both engaging in an act of independence and attempting to secure justice. The point is, doing something for personal gain is not necessarily wrong. But it is inherently self-centered. The difficulty is not in determining the motive behind an act of independence but in counting the cost: Is it, indeed, for our own good?

Remembering the case of the battered wife, we must begin with the assumption that some acts of independence are for our own good. The person who is exploited is doing no one any good by enduring the abuse. In such cases, independence is a preferable alternative to a relationship that denigrates both partners and cheapens the meaning of human life.

But when is a relationship truly exploitive? And how do we determine when an act of independence is justified? These are extremely difficult questions, not simply because they are subjective, but because we live in a society that encourages us to make self-centered choices. We are constantly bombarded with the message that nothing is more important than our own personal happiness. We are told to act, buy, and live as if nothing else mattered. As a result, acts of independence are assumed to be right *whenever* they make us happy.

The Christian needs to keep two things in mind about the modern fascination with self. First, a self-centered life not only contradicts a central Christian ethic but it also violates God's creational plan for our lives. In simple terms, our preoccupation with self isn't good for us. We don't find our fulfillment in ourselves, we find it in our Creator. That's why our first obligation is to love God and then our neighbor (Deut. 6:5; Lev. 19:18; Matt. 22:37–40). It's through the gift of love that we receive our greatest joy.

This simple truth isn't easy for twentieth-century Christians to grasp. For one thing, most people in our world don't believe it, and modern Christians find it difficult to reject popular opinion. A good example of this is the way some among us have taken the command "love your neighbor as yourself" and turned it into a *love yourself* theology. For two millennia, Christians have taken the command to love your neighbor as yourself at face value. The phrase "as yourself" was assumed to be a barometer of sorts, defining the quality of such love. How should I act toward my neighbor? At least as graciously as I act toward myself. Until our era, self-love was not taken as a biblical command but an assumption about human nature. Today, drawing our sustenance from the narcissistic waters of our age, we've made it the "chief duty of man."

The second thing we ought to remember is that while all acts of independence are not wrong, the desire for independence itself is rooted in sin. Indeed, the first act of disobedience recorded in Genesis is motivated by the desire to become like God (Gen. 3:5). The meaning here, of course, is not to emulate God in a positive way but to become independent of his will. From that moment on, humans have sought to secure their own comfort and well being, to satisfy themselves. It hasn't worked, of course, but humans haven't been quick to learn from history.

Independence, then, is humanism in its most ribald, individualistic form. It's the desire to live a life of self-control, to put one's self at the center of the universe. Independence declares that I don't need God or others, that I'm the maker of my own destiny. Independence assumes that self-satisfaction is the fundamental criterion for behavior and that it can be achieved independently of the wills of others. Independence admits to no needs, except the need to play god.

**When Is Independence Good?**

With this in mind, let's raise again the question: When are acts of independence genuinely "for our own good"? Our first answer must be: rarely. Most acts of independence are rooted in our desire to control, to acquire a level of freedom that human beings weren't designed to have. Thus, though our independence seems to be in our interest, we find its satisfaction fleeting, its consequences tragic, like the fruit of the forbidden tree. Instead of being fulfilled, we find ourselves locked out of the

Garden for which we were created. Abandoned and helpless.

There is one exception, however, and with it we arrive at a second answer: An act of independence can be for our own good when it is grounded—not in our own self-interest—but in our love for God. At first blush, this may sound like double-talk, so let me explain.

Our first priority, remember, must be to love God. All other concerns must bend to this one. The reason is not that Christians are masochists or unconcerned about themselves but that they believe loving God will ultimately be for the good of all, including themselves. Our first concern, therefore, is not to avoid acts of independence but to love and honor our Creator, doing what is good and right in his eyes. Thus, an act of independence is justified—indeed, is the right thing to do—when it truly honors God.

For example, I think that heresies do not honor God. Therefore, in spite of the importance I attach to stable church relationships, a heretical church should not be endured forever.[10] If I find that I'm being bombarded by lies from the pulpit and all my attempts to correct the problem end in failure, I'll have no choice but to leave the church. The need for community does not supersede my obligation to love God. In saying this, of course, I'm putting myself squarely within the tradition of those— like Abraham and Paul—who decided that their first obligation was to obey God rather than other people.

The problem is that most acts of independence today are not like that. Indeed, the whole notion of obeying God rather than others sounds archaic, if not insane, in our world. That's because the modern world has reversed those priorities. It's not the glory of God that moves us, it's the splendor of the self. And thus, irony of ironies, it turns out that the only justifiable reason for an act of independence is itself unreasonable in the modern world.

## Conclusion

For the Christian in the modern world, acts of independence ought to be the exception, not the rule. Flights of freedom are almost always a tragedy. Even when they are necessary, they testify to the pervasive influence of sin. The message that we in the West need to hear is not that acts of independence are sometimes needed but that they are always painful. Even the most righteous act of independence is destined to promote forsakenness and despair. And few such acts, these days, are the least bit righteous.

The question is, how do we build a world where abandonment is the exception rather than the rule? In the language of this book, how do we redeem a society bent on its own dissolution? We begin by resisting the spirit of our age. At the outset we must remember that we live in a world where self-indulgence is normative and where relational freedom is considered a right. As long as we share these values, we will not be a part of the solution to the problem of forsakenness. We will be the problem.

To be sure, the task before us is a formidable one. The spirit of independence lives not only around us but also within us. It's our own desire to put self-satisfaction on the throne that permits this spirit to have its way with us. Until that occupant of the throne is removed, we'll have no victory. Until the imposter king steps down, our doom is sure. "Love the Lord your God with all your heart and with all your soul and with all your mind. This is the first and greatest commandment. And the second is like it: Love your neighbor as yourself." The battle against the spirit of independence begins here. Or it has no beginning.

# A PARABLE OF CHOICE

||||||||||||||||||||||||||||||||||||||||||||||||||||||||||||||||||||||||||||||||||||||||||||||||||||||||||||||||||||||||

Sometimes it can be discouraging to look at the social factors that lead to forsakenness. They seem so large and abstract that we are tempted to think we can do nothing about them. That is a fiction due in large part to my colleagues in the social sciences, who describe societies as *things* and *forces* largely out of our control. In a sense they are right, of course. Social conditions do have tremendous power and influence over our lives. But in another sense, they are profoundly wrong. Societies are the creations of human beings. All of us, together, make choices that collectively give rise to the societies in which we live. What that means is that if you and I make different choices, we can change not only ourselves but also the world in which we and others live.

This has been a book about choices. In fact, we can say that the argument of this book can be boiled down to a single choice: *How will we handle rejection and loss when it invades our lives?* What will you and I do with our experiences of forsakenness? They'll come, we can be sure of that. The world we live in makes that inevitable. What is not inevitable, however, is our response to those experiences. That is when we'll make our choices. And that is when we'll write our own stories of redemption, or otherwise.

So I thought it might be good to leave you with a story as well. It is a children's story, but it was written for children of all ages. It did not happen. But it's happening every day.

# 8

## *Chris and the Cane*

Chris Chun wasn't an ordinary boy.

Oh, he had dirt under his fingernails and floppy shoelaces, just like other boys. And he loved double-decker ice cream cones, water puddles on Sunday morning, and Saturdays all day long.

But Chris wasn't an ordinary boy because he actually *enjoyed* helping others. When his father shoveled snow in the winter, Chris loved to shovel right by his side. When Grandpa Chun wanted someone to walk to town with him, Chris was always the first to volunteer. And when his little sister bumped her head or scraped her knee, Chris would be there in a flash, with hugs, sympathy, and Band-Aids.

Chris wasn't perfect, of course. He complained about naps, interrupted his parents' conversations, and sometimes offered advice when it wasn't needed or appreciated. Once, he even stole twenty-five cents from his father's change box, just so he could buy candy. But Chris was always sorry when he was caught. And on any given day, he could be sorry a hundred times or more.

No, Chris wasn't perfect. Or ordinary. Chris Chun was very helpful.

One day at school, Chris noticed a boy sitting under a big elm tree at recess. He'd never seen the boy before, but he knew something was wrong. Few boys sat down at recess, and no one sat down alone. Chris thought about going over to see what the trouble was. But he was in the middle of a soccer game, and soccer was his favorite sport. "What should I do?" thought Chris. He decided to keep playing. Even Chris Chun wasn't that helpful.

Later that day, however, when Chris was walking home from school, he saw the boy again. Only this time he wasn't sitting under the elm. He was walking down the sidewalk. But he was still alone. Chris didn't hesitate for a moment.

"Hi, I'm Chris," he panted, as he ran to catch up with him. "Are you new at school?"

"Yeah," said the boy. "We just moved here a few days ago. My name's Jake."

In a minute, Chris knew exactly what Jake's problem was. It was the same problem he'd had when his family first moved to town. Jake was missing his old friends back home, and he was feeling lonely. Right then and there, Chris decided to help. He promised himself that he would become Jake's friend.

Well, Chris lived up to his promise. In the weeks and months that followed, Chris made Jake his number-one priority. He walked to and from school with Jake every day, even though it meant going over a mile out of his way. He asked Jake to play on his neighborhood soccer team, even though Jake lived in another neighborhood. He even managed to get Jake invited into his club, even though the club wasn't officially open to new members.

Well, it wasn't long before Jake and Chris became close friends. Jake completely forgot about his loneliness as well as the companions he'd left behind.

But then something happened that Chris didn't understand. Not at all. One day when he went to pick up Jake on his way to school, he discovered that Jake had already left—without him. When he got to school, he noticed that Jake was playing soccer, but on another team. And when he sat beside Jake in the library later that day, Jake hardly said a word. He just did his work and left, without even saying good-bye.

At first, Chris thought that maybe Jake was having problems at home. But usually when that happened, Jake would want to talk about it. This time Jake didn't want to talk. Not about anything. In fact, as the days went along, it became pretty clear that Jake was making an effort to ignore Chris altogether. Jake was not depressed. Jake was having a good time. But he was having it with other people.

Finally Chris understood. Jake had rejected him for another set of friends. Chris Chun was crushed. Quite literally. His head fell. His shoulders began to slump. And his helpful spirit . . . well, his helpful spirit seemed to have been squeezed right out of him. Everybody noticed it. Chris Chun changed.

Chris did not change into an awful person, though. In fact, if you hadn't known Chris before, you would think he was a pretty nice guy. He didn't get into fights on the playground. He didn't stop doing his homework. And he didn't take his disappointment out on his family. Indeed, some would say that he had even become a better boy, for he stopped interrupting his parents' conversations and never again offered advice where it wasn't needed.

No, it wasn't that Chris became bad. It was that Chris became—for the first time in his life—a regular boy. He didn't bother those who didn't bother him. But he didn't go out of his way to help, either. Chris Chun had become ordinary.

It wasn't long before people began to accept the new Chris. Some said the change was actually a good thing: that Chris had finally grown up. His counselor at school felt that he was just going through a difficult stage in his life, and there was really nothing to worry about.

But one person knew better. He was Chris's grandfather, a hearty old man of about eighty-five, who lived as if he were forty but spoke as if he'd lived forever. Anyway, when Grandpa Chun saw the new Chris, he knew something significant had happened—not just to him, but in him. And regardless of how the change might be explained by helpful friends and local do-gooders, Grandpa Chun knew for a fact that the change was not good.

Now Grandpa Chun was a great storyteller. And every Sunday after church when the whole Chun family gathered for dinner, Grandpa Chun would entertain all the children with his stories. For over twenty years, his Sunday routine never varied. The minute dinner was over, the children would start to beg Grandpa to tell them a story. For a while (it seemed an eternity), he wouldn't say a thing. He'd just sit there, smiling, listening to the children plead.

Finally, he would "give in," lumber over to the overstuffed chair in the living room, and make himself comfortable. The children would do the same, spreading themselves out on the floor, encircling Grandpa Chun with their bodies and their expectations.

One Sunday, however, Grandpa did something a little different. For one thing, he asked Chris to sit with him in the overstuffed chair (which wasn't easy, by the way;

Grandpa was a bit overstuffed himself). For another, he gave his story a title, which he didn't usually do, mostly because he didn't know what his stories were going to be about until he told them. But this time was different. This time he knew exactly what the story was about as well as for whom the story was told. He called it, "The Cane."

"Once upon a time," he said, "there was a Mastercraftsman, who lived in the land of Nevaeh. Now the unusual thing about this Mastercraftsman is that everything he made was beautiful, and nothing he made was ever alike. Not only did each piece look unique, but each of his creations was designed for a different purpose. So instead of making hundreds of cuckoo clocks that looked just alike and did the same thing, he made only one cuckoo clock, and it was very beautiful.

"One of his many creations was a walking cane. And never before was there a cane such as this. It was made of a wood so hard that a three-hundred-pound man could put his full weight on it and it wouldn't even bend. Its grip was comfortable. Its peg held fast to the ground. And its grain was so finely polished that when you held the cane before your eyes, you could see not only your own reflection but also deep into the wood itself.

"One day, the Mastercraftsman said to the cane, 'It's time for you to get to work. I know of a boy who has been in an accident. One of his legs has been badly hurt, and he can't walk without assistance. I want you to become the boy's assistance. With your help, that boy will walk again.'

"The cane was overjoyed. This was what it had longed to do. When the boy received the cane, he was overjoyed as well. He placed the cane in his right hand, pressed it to

the floor, and for the first time since the accident, walked
without the help of other people. At first, of course, the
boy moved carefully, not wanting to fall and not being
sure of the cane's strength. But as he used the cane, he
learned he could rely upon it. As his confidence grew, so
did his ambition. He began to walk faster and faster, and
he pushed the cane harder and harder. But the cane was
equal to his ambition. And the boy was able to move
back into the mainstream of life.

"One day, however, the boy went to see the doctor.
And when he returned, he was walking—without the
help of his cane. At first, the cane was happy to see the
boy walking on his own. But after a few days, the cane
began to feel lonely. It missed the companionship of the
boy and the tight grip of the boy's fingers around its
handle.

"And then, something really awful happened. The
cane was feeling so lonely that it decided to try to get the
boy's attention. Whenever a door closed or someone
jumped up and down upstairs, the cane used the vibra-
tions to move closer and closer to the edge of the shelf on
which it had been placed. Eventually, the cane managed
to fall off the shelf, landing right in front of the boy's
bedroom door. The cane was pleased, knowing the boy
would see it the minute he came through the door.

"But when the boy came into his room, he didn't see
the cane; he tripped over it instead. And when he picked
himself up from his fall, he was angry. He grabbed the
cane by its throat, accused it of unspeakable deeds, and
ran out the back door of the house. When he reached the
edge of his yard, he cocked the cane back like a javelin,
and threw it as far as he possibly could, yelling as it
sailed through the air, 'Get out of my life, cane! I don't

need you any more! I don't need you any more!' The cane
landed in a ditch. Its finish was unharmed, but its spirit
was broken.

"Now the Mastercraftsman never lost track of his
creations. He knew exactly what had happened to the
cane. And so the minute it hit the ground, the Mastercraftsman left his shop and went looking for the cane.
But the cane had forgotten about the Mastercraftsman.
Forgotten about who had made it. Forgotten, too, for
what purpose it had been made. All it could remember
was the boy's tight grip and the words of rejection as it
went sailing out of the boy's life.

"When the Mastercraftsman found the cane, he took it
back to his workplace. He cleaned it off, polished its
surface, and hung it near the front window of his shop.
The cane looked beautiful again. And everyone who
walked by the shop admired its beauty.

"Within a few days, the Mastercraftsman asked the
cane if it was ready to go back to work. But the cane said
'No, I don't ever want to go back. I want to remain in
your shop, on display.'

" 'But you won't be happy here,' said the Mastercraftsman.

" 'Why?' said the cane.

" 'Because I didn't make you for display,' said the
Mastercraftsman.

"But the cane didn't listen. It wanted to be safe. And
so it stayed on display in the front window. Every day
people came into the workshop, admired its beauty, and
wanted to buy it. But the Mastercraftsman said it wasn't
for sale. And the cane felt good. Sort of.

"Then one day a feeble old man with a bad limp came
into the shop. He said his crutch of twenty years had

broken. Because he was poor, he didn't think he could afford to replace it. Without the crutch, however, he couldn't take walks in the morning or go shopping by himself or see his grandchildren across town. And so he wondered if the Mastercraftsman had an old, second-hand crutch in the shop; something he could use for the few remaining years of his life.

"The Mastercraftsman didn't say a word. He simply reached up, pulled the cane down from the display rack, and placed it in the old man's hands. For a long time, the old man looked at the cane, admiring its deep grain and perfect finish. Then he set it down. 'I couldn't take this,' he said. 'This is the most beautiful cane I've ever seen. A cane like this belongs in the hands of kings and queens. It doesn't belong with a poor old man like me. Besides, someone of wealth will one day pay you a handsome price for it.'

" 'You are wrong about that,' said the Mastercraftsman. 'This cane is not for sale. It's far too valuable to be purchased. But you are right when you say you can't take the cane. The cane can neither be purchased nor taken. It must be given. And it must come to you of its own accord.'

"Then, the Mastercraftsman picked up the cane, walked to the back of his shop, and held the cane close to his heart. 'Are you willing to go with the old man, my cane?' he said. 'Are you willing to go and live the life for which you were created?'

" 'I make you this promise,' continued the Master-craftsman. 'If you stay on display, you may be admired and you may gain a great reputation for your beauty, but it will not make you happy. In fact, your insides will begin to rot. And over time, even your gleaming surface will start to crack. In the end, your beauty will disappear altogether, and you will be cast aside in favor of canes that are younger and more beautiful than you.

" 'But if you become this man's cane, you'll never gain a great reputation. Few people will probably ever know of you. The old man is feeble. He'll knock you against corners and lampposts, and your surface will become tarnished and chipped. But with every chip, your fibers will gain strength. With every stain, your insides will grow more beautiful. And because of you, the old man will walk. His world will be enlarged through your existence. And you will be happy. Forever.' "

Grandpa Chun drew a deep breath, hesitated, and then stopped. The children, whose eyes were riveted on their Grandpa, waited. But Grandpa said nothing.

"What happened?" said one of the children finally. "What did the cane do?"

"I don't know," said Grandpa.

"You don't know?" blurted another child in disbelief. "What do you mean, Grandpa? You *must* know!"

"I'm sorry," said Grandpa, "but I don't know what happened to the cane. You see, the end of the story hasn't yet been written."

"Oh Grandpa, please, please," said the children. "Please make up an ending. We want to find out what happened! We want to know what choice the cane made!"

Grandpa let out a sigh. "So do I, my children, so do I."

Chris Chun didn't join the chorus of pleas, however. And he didn't move from the chair. The other children, now convinced that Grandpa wouldn't finish his story, slowly drifted out of the room. But Chris stayed put.

Finally, when everyone else had gone, Chris let his head fall against his Grandpa's chest.

"Grandpa," Chris whispered, "Grandpa, do you think the Mastercraftsman is a little like God?"

"Oh no . . . I don't think so," said Grandpa. "Well, maybe just a little."

"And Grandpa," continued Chris, "am I . . . am I a little like the cane?"

"Oh no . . . I don't think so," repeated Grandpa. "Well, maybe just a little."

Tears began to well up in Chris's eyes. Grandpa wrapped his big powerful arm around Chris' shoulder. Neither of them said another word. They just sat there. Together. And cried.

Chris was never the same after that. Never the same ordinary boy he had become, that is. Oh, he still had floppy shoelaces and dirt under his fingernails. But he was unusual, nevertheless.

For one thing, he regained his helpful disposition. And right there, that set him apart from most. But Chris regained something else as well. His old spirit. You could see it in the way he attacked life. From the moment he shot out of bed in the morning until he laid his head down at night, Chris was on the move. He seemed to give one hundred percent of himself to every minute in the day. In fact, people said Chris was a lot like his grandpa.

But the story of Chris Chun, like the story of the cane, is not yet complete. Chris, after all, is still young. Before him lie trials and temptations he can't imagine, opportunities of which he can't even dream. But though the contours of his future remain a mystery, the promise of the Mastercraftsman still holds true:

"Whoever wants to save his life will lose it, but whoever loses his life for me will find it. What good is it for a man to gain the whole world, and yet lose or forfeit his very self?"

# Notes

||||||||||||||||||||||||||||||||||||||||||||||||||||||||||||||||||||||||||||||||||||||||||||||||||||||

## Chapter 2

1. Webster's dictionary (*Webster's New World Dictionary of the American Language,* ed. D. B. Guralnik [New York, NY: World Pub. Co., 1972]) defines a stigma as "something that detracts from the character or reputation of a person, group, etc.; mark of disgrace or reproach." It's a Latin word, which derives its origin from the Greek, meaning "to prick with a pointed instrument." The base word is "stick," indicating the process by which the stigma is received.

2. D. Stanley Eitzen (*In Conflict and Order* [Boston, MA: Allyn and Bacon, 1982]) defines stigma as "a label of social disgrace" (p. 503). "The labeling school suggests that the other person's peculiarity has not caused us to regard him as different so much as our labeling hypothesis has caused his peculiarity" (p. 222). This is fairly typical and shows the modern sociologist's deterministic inclinations. The labeling notion emphasizes collective responsibility only. It fails to take individual accountability seriously. Nevertheless, since no one wants to be stigmatized, it's not incorrect to say that "others" place the stigma on the receiver, and in that sense, the modern sociologist puts the emphasis in the right place. Both the labelers and the receivers, however, make choices—for which they are responsible—that enable stigmatizing to persist.

3. This emphasis on intelligence and beauty is clearly a problem when it comes to child rearing (James Dobson, *Hide and Seek,* [Old Tappan, New Jersey: Revell, 1974]). I don't wish to give the impression that ours is the only society that emphasizes these two qualities, however. Indeed, they are universally valued traits; that is why bodily adornment, hair styling, and education are found in nearly all cultures (see John Friedl, *Cultural Anthropology* [New York, NY: Harper & Row, 1976], pp. 46–52). But what

*141*

differentiates American society from others is, first, our preoccupation with intelligence and beauty, and second, their importance in status achievement. Because they are so highly valued, they have become the primary means to upward mobility. Thus, those possessing them have a substantial advantage in the competition for success. (In terms of corporate success, it seems to help men more than women; see M. E. Heilman and M. H. Stopeck, "Attractiveness and Corporate Success: Differential Causal Attributions for Males and Females," *Journal of Applied Psychology*, 70 [1985]: 379–88; see also B. Major, et al., "Physical Attractiveness and Self-Esteem," *Personality and Social Psychology Bulletin*, 10 [1984]: 43–50).

4. *The Scarlet Letter*, by Nathaniel Hawthorne, offers a very good introduction to the meaning and implications of stigmas, by the way. Hawthorne has a deep understanding of the way in which people can feel trapped by their social roles and circumstances. This is evident in *The House of Seven Gables* as well.

5. Thus, I can now see *The Elephant Man* and mention it in books. And, I must say, I'm glad. I learned that the first time I snuck out of the house to see a movie. Since I was already doing something wrong, I figured I might as well do something *really* wrong, so I went to see *The Days of Wine and Roses*. Prepared to have the wonders of the world paraded before me in all their awful splendor, I was dumbfounded to be confronted with one of the most powerful messages on alcoholism I had ever encountered. I came to the theater, looking for sin and got a sermon instead.

6. I trust my readers aren't offended by this comment. Calling whites "people without color" is a modest attempt at turning a stigma on its head. Blacks in North America have been subjected to all kinds of pejorative labels over the years. Not too long ago, calling a black person "colored" was considered polite. That term went into disrepute with the black power movement of the 1960s. Nevertheless, it strikes me that when whites called blacks "colored," whites were by implication calling themselves "colorless." Since most of us want to be thought of as colorful people, the use of the term by the majority group was a bit of an irony. I am indebted to Joe Lloyd, Assistant Dean of Students at Gordon College, for this observation. For a discussion of racial labels, see J. E. Williams and J. R. Stabler, "If White Means Good, Then Black . . . " *Psychology Today* (July, 1973): 51–54 and "Reversing the Bigotry of Language," *Psychology Today* (March, 1974): 34.

7. The literature on the relationship between self-image and the attitudes of others is not conclusive, but there seems to be evidence that my friend's reaction was not atypical. The expectations of others do influence our own estimates of ourselves and our behavior. The classic study here, of course, is *Pygmalion in*

*the Classroom* by Robert Rosenthal and Lenore Jacobson (New York, NY: Holt, 1968). Its results remain somewhat controversial, however. Regardless of the merits of the "self-fulfilling prophecy" when applied to the classroom, few of us would doubt the influence of others upon our self-esteem, especially in the early years of our development (see D. M. Bush and R. G. Simmons, "Socialization over the Life Course" and Morris Rosenberg, "The Self-Concept: Social Product and Social Force" in *Social Psychology*, ed. M. Rosenberg and R. Turner [New York, NY: Basic, 1981]; also see Tamotsu Shibutani, *Society and Personality* [Englewood Cliffs, NJ: Prentice-Hall, 1961], pp. 432–470).

8. This is the idea of the "looking-glass self" developed by Charles Horton Cooley in *Human Nature and the Social Order* (New York, NY: Charles Scribner's Sons, 1922). It says that we come to understand ourselves—who we are—in the mirror of social interaction. This idea has value, I think, but can be over-exaggerated. Though we learn about ourselves through others, one of the things we learn as we grow is to ferret out what we ought to believe and what we should not. Thus, we learn to be discriminating viewers of the "looking-glass self"—some people more successfully than others.

9. Another famous sociologist, George Herbert Mead, developed a conception of self-understanding similar to Cooley's concept, but Mead's is oriented more to the human tendency of role playing. One of his ideas (see *Mind, Self and Society* [Chicago, IL: University of Chicago Press, 1934]) was that we often play the role of the other, putting ourselves in the shoes of those around us, and then seeing ourselves from their perspective. Erving Goffman, who has done much to provide us with a sociological understanding of stigma (*Stigma* [Englewood Cliffs, NJ: Prentice-Hall, 1963]), was greatly influenced by Mead (as seen especially in *The Presentation of Self in Everyday Life* [Garden City, NY: Double-day Anchor, 1959]).

10. It should come as no surprise that those with higher education are usually more adept at perceiving what is considered appropriate language. This accounts, in part, for why education is negatively correlated with racial prejudice in most survey research; the highly educated are better at selecting the least prejudicial response (J. F. Dittes, "Psychology of Religion," *The Handbook of Social Psychology*, ed. Lindzey and Aronson [Reading, MA: Addison-Wesley, 1968]; G.W. Alport and J. M. Ross, "Personal Religious Orientation and Prejudice," *Journal of Personality and Social Psychology*, 5 [1967]: 432–443; A. L. Rosenblum, "Social Class Affiliation and Ethnic Prejudice," *International Journal of Comparative Sociology*, 8 [1967]: 245–264). For a similar reason, educated people are likely to shun

crass labels ("she's bonkers"), trading them in for more pleasant ones ("she's unpredictable"). Like prejudice, however, stigmatizing is a matter not of refinement but of meaning. And regardless of the terms used, both the victim and the stigmatizer know perfectly well their intent. Thus, the effects of stigmas remain substantially the same, regardless of the words chosen.

11. This, of course, is how stereotypes sometimes develop. We see someone behave in a certain way (rob a store), fixate upon a certain aspect of that person (blond hair), and generalize the behavior trait to a certain population (blond people are petty criminals). Such reasoning is so patently absurd, however, that it can be sustained only in a certain social context. That context usually includes (1) an assumed social problem (store robberies are getting out of hand), (2) an inability to deal with the problem (the police can't cope), and (3) a search for a hidden, simple solution (we have too many blond-haired people). According to the frustration-aggression thesis (John Dollard, Neal Miller, Leonard Doob, *Frustration and Aggression* [New Haven, CT: Yale, 1939]), it's nourished by people who are exasperated with life in general and are, therefore, looking for a reason for their frustration. For a review of the literature, see G. E. Simpson and J. M. Yinger, *Racial and Cultural Minorities: An Analysis of Prejudice and Discrimination* (New York, NY: Harper & Row, 1972), pp. 63–102.

12. Notice the "projection" involved in my thinking. I took that which I feared in myself, stupidity, and projected it on others. This is by no means unusual. Projection is often associated with prejudice, the classic study here being John Dollard's *Caste and Class in a Southern Town* (New Haven, CT: Yale, 1937). Note two things about prejudice stemming from projection. First, it may in fact help stigmatizers control their behavior; by pointing out the stupidity of others, my awareness of stupid statements may be heightened, and I might be less likely to utter them myself. Second, however, because the reason for my prejudice is something I fear in myself, my prejudice will not be affected by external events. Thus, everyone in my community might stop making stupid statements, but I would go right on trying to find them. In that sense, I have created a need for prejudice within myself.

13. This is really a status game based upon stigma. By stigmatizing others for a trait I don't possess, I gain a certain amount of status. A vivid description of this phenomenon is presented in Lillian Smith's *Killers of the Dream* (New York, NY: W. W. Norton, 1978). She shows why some of the most rabid racism in the Old South was associated with lower-class whites, even though they were nearly as poor and abused as blacks. White skin was their

only claim to fame; it was the only thing between them and the lowest group on the totem pole. Thus, to protect their ounce of status, they would do everything in their power to keep blacks in their place. Smith's book, which is essentially autobiographical, is a must for those who wish to understand the dynamics of prejudice and bigotry.

# *Chapter 3*

1. Of the many good books available on this topic, some deal directly with particular philosophical issues, while others are concerned simply with coming to terms with the experience itself. Some of the more readable are: C. S. Lewis, *The Problem of Pain* (New York, NY: Macmillan, 1962); Philip Yancey, *Where Is God When It Hurts?* (Grand Rapids, MI: Zondervan, 1978) and Edith Schaeffer, *Affliction* (Old Tappan, NJ: Revell, 1978).

2. It's hard to read the Bible without coming to the conclusion that there's an over-arching, this-worldly justice built into God's creation. Proverbs and the Psalms, in particular, are loaded with assurances that, in the long run, sin leads to trouble and right living leads to God's blessing. The problem is—and what Eliphaz forgot is—the timing of such justice is unknown to us. The Evil One has his way for awhile, just as he did with Job. For some, such as the baby who dies of famine, that interlude may last a lifetime. For others, it may be a day, a year, or four score and seven. We simply don't know. It's our ignorance of such matters that ought to make us careful about uttering judgments like Eliphaz's.

3. This doesn't mean that it's the right question to ask, by the way. It only means that asking it is a virtual certainty. Frankly, I don't know what God thinks of such questions. On the one hand, the final chapters of Job (Job 38–41) indicate that God wasn't altogether pleased with Job's questions and that Job, after hearing God's rebuke, felt that through his questions he had sinned (42:1–6). On the other hand, the Bible is loaded with such questions, which often come from God's most loyal servants (David and Habakkuk, for example). Regardless of what God thinks of them, then, such questions have and will be asked. As far as I'm concerned, I couldn't be honest with God and fail to ask them. But, like Job, once I see God's perspective on the matter, honesty may also require that I ask forgiveness.

4. This shouldn't be taken as an assertion that pain is undeserved. In a general sense, all pain is deserved, as it is the fruit of Adam and

Eve's sin. Here, however, we are talking about a particular pain, and saying that it may not be warranted in a particular situation. The statement, moreover, is conditional: *If* one assumes that a particular pain is undeserved, *then* its existence can't be blamed on the one who feels it. The assumption, of course, could be wrong.

5. The first comprehensive account of Greek religion comes from the epic poems attributed to Homer, the *Iliad* and the *Odyssey*. Many of the gods in the Greek pantheon show up in these stories, including Zeus, Apollo, and Aphrodite. Though no systematic body of theology ever developed, through Greek literature and drama, one can gain a fairly clear picture of Greek metaphysical assumptions during the classical period. The most apparent characteristic of Greek gods is their anthropomorphic nature. They are like human beings, only physically superior and immortal. As such, they play favorites, have rivalries, and intervene in human affairs on the basis of whim and human emotion. Though some gods seek justice, as do some humans, there is no guarantee that their actions will bring about that end. Like Agamemnon in Aeschylus's trilogy, *Oresteia*, the gods themselves are faced with difficult choices; they may intervene to give justice a nudge (as does Athena), but they are powerless to correct the overall human picture—or to deal with the problem of pain.

6. For a discussion of the problem of evil as grounds for disbelief in God, see John Hick, *Philosophy of Religion* (Englewood Cliffs, NJ: Prentice-Hall, 1963).

7. Though this may seem like a strange option, it is a highly efficient means of dealing with both the problem of pain and forsakenness. By denying the ultimate reality of all things physical, a pantheist (for example) can at the same time deny the reality of pain and proclaim a cosmic oneness in the spiritual world (reality). To overcome pain, one merely must overcome the illusion of material existence and unite with the one spiritual reality. The result—no more pain or forsakenness. One pays a price for this solution, however. One must also deny the reality of physical pleasure—as well as the God of creation who declared, "It is good."

8. For a discussion of the theodicy issue from a sociological perspective, see Peter Berger's *Sacred Canopy* (Garden City, NY: Doubleday, 1969), pp. 53–80. Tracing the sociological development of theodicy in Judaism and Christianity (and others), Berger notes the crucial nature of this problem in modern societies. In contrast to the position taken here, however, he suggests it results from a breakdown in the plausibility structure in modern societies. His explanation, though, is not incompatible with the

one presented here since economic conditions are surely a major contributor to the nature of modern social structure.

9. According to Tom Sine (*The Mustard Seed Conspiracy* [Waco, TX: Word, 1981]), most of the people in the third world live in "degrading situations" by Western standards. "Seventy million people . . . are in imminent danger of starvation. . . . Four hundred million are chronically malnourished, and fully one billion don't get anything like enough to eat. Two billion, or almost half the world's people, make less than two hundred dollars per person per year" (p. 32).

10. Phrase, as well as understanding, was taken from Sheldon Vanauken, *A Severe Mercy* (San Francisco, CA: Harper & Row, 1977).

# *Chapter 4*

1. Lifted directly from C. S. Lewis, *A Grief Observed* (London: Faber and Faber, 1964).

2. See, for example, I. O. Glick, R. S. Weiss, and C. M. Parks, *The First Year of Bereavement* (New York, NY: Wiley, 1974).

3. See R. Fulton, "Death, Grief, and Social Recuperation," *Omega: Journal of Death and Dying* (1970): 23–28. He differentiates between *high-grief death* and *low-grief death*. The latter tend to be anticipated deaths; foreknowledge, he says, enables us to go through depression, heightened concern for the ill persons, rehearsal of the death, and adjustment to the consequences of the death. Richard Schulz (*The Psychology of Death, Dying and Bereavement* [Reading, MA: Addison-Wesley, 1978]) disagrees that early depression relieves the impact of guilt, citing the work of C. M. Borstein, et al. ("The Depression of Widowhood After Thirteen Months," *British Journal of Psychiatry* [1973]: 561–566) for support.

4. I'm referring here to the possibility of emotional adjustment. Certainly it's possible to partially anticipate the consequences of the death of a well person; that's why we have wills, buy flight insurance, name godparents, and so on. In doing this, we're preparing for an unanticipated death. But, it's unlikely that sane people will want daily to anticipate the deaths of all significant people in their lives.

5. Schulz (*The Psychology of Death, Dying and Bereavement*) discusses this phenomenon; in doing so, it's not clear if he is here drawing upon Fulton ("Death, Grief, and Social Recuperation"),

Glick, et al. (*First Year of Bereavement*), or his own wisdom. Regardless, it does constitute wisdom, I think.

6. Lest one think I am trying to be cute here, let me state in earnest: 1) that I'm confident she is with the Lord; 2) that heaven is appropriately called a "home"; and 3) that she is more satisfied now than ever before. I used the phrase "going home to be with the Lord," moreover, not to avoid the word "died," but to capture grandma's spirit. Readers who are offended by its use should reevaluate their taste.

7. Fulton, "Death, Grief, and Social Recuperation." Regardless of the cause, grief clearly takes a toll. The "Broken Heart" idea (C. M. Parkes, "The Broken Heart," *Death: Current Perspectives*, ed. E. S. Shneidman [Palo Alto, CA: Mayfield, 1976]), which links grief with higher mortality rates, is the most arresting. Though the notion that grief might cause death is an old one (in 1657, Dr. Heberden's Bill listed grief as the cause of ten deaths [Parkes, "The Broken Heart," p. 333]), a large number of contemporary researchers have substantiated the claim. See P. R. Cox and J. R. Ford, "The Mortality of Widows Shortly After Widowhood," *Social Demography*, ed. T. Ford and G. F. De Jong (Englewood Cliffs, NJ: Prentice-Hall, 1970); M. Young, B. Bernard, and C. Wallis, "The Mortality of Widowers," *Social Demography*; J. Mathison, "A Cross-cultural View of Widowhood," *Omega: Journal of Death and Dying* (1970): 201–218; and B. Schoenberg, "A Survey of the Advice of Physicians for the Bereaved," *General Practitioner* (1969): 105–110.

8. This reflects a male cultural ideal that discourages emotional displays, even during times of mourning (R. J. Kastenbaum, *Death, Society, and Human Experience* [St. Louis, MO: C. V. Mosby, 1977], pp. 260-263). In my case, it also reflects an inability to verbalize strongly felt emotions; interestingly, I have no difficulty expressing them on paper or demonstrating them with a hug or a tear. But well-articulated phrases simply won't come to me. Pathologies of that sort have their good side, by the way. I'm convinced that one of my motives for writing is to say in print something I couldn't have verbalized in a million years.

9. See M. Learner, "When, Why, and Where People Die," *Death: Current Perspectives*.

10. I still like David Riesman's demographics of industrialization in *The Lonely Crowd* (New Haven, CT: Yale, 1950).

11. I've attempted an explanation of the relationship between modernity and community in my book *Belonging* (Grand Rapids, MI: Zondervan, 1985). In general, we moderns simply don't have many long-term, durable relationships in our lives, and that's true within both family and church. This makes death less

visible (the point of this paragraph) and grief more difficult to endure (the point of the next paragraph).

12. A fuller discussion of the grief-forsakenness phenomenon, for example, would require more anthropological and psychological insight. Cultures handle grief differently (see Arnold Toynbee, "Various Ways in Which Human Beings Have Sought to Reconcile Themselves to the Fact of Death," *Death: Current Perspectives*), for one thing, and one ought not assume that Western grief forms are typical. Psychologists, too, have speculated widely on the causes of grief. Freud, for example, felt that mourning was a process that enabled the griever to overcome the denial of death and to withdraw from the deceased (*Mourning and Melancholia*). Thus, he assumed grief was functional for the survivor. Bowlby ("Process of Mourning," *International Journal of Psychoanalysis* [1961]: 317), on the other hand, felt that grieving was an attempt to remain close to the deceased and thus was not helpful in recovery. I suspect they were both partially correct (to put it positively), depending upon the intervention of individual, environmental, and providential circumstances.

13. Some helpful books about this issue include Michael Leming and George Dickinson, *Understanding Death, Dying and Bereavement* (NY: Rinehart & Winston, 1985); C. S. Lewis, *A Grief Observed*; and Joe Bayly, *The View from the Hearse* (Elgin, IL: David C. Cook, 1969).

14. My father had a terrific sense of humor, and his responsible side did not obviate laughter. The picture I want to paint here is not of a man without humor but of someone whose sense of responsibility was so strong that it sometimes overburdened him. Nevertheless, he had a quick wit, and when he was in the mood, he could be the life of the party. I think he felt a little guilty about it afterward, however.

15. Note the correlation between my conception of God and of my father. Freud and Durkheim would have a field day with this observation, since both of them saw our images of God being shaped by our conceptions of human reality (society for Durkheim, ancestors for Freud). If one doesn't begin one's analysis of religion with the assumption that "God is," then one's deductions are perfectly reasonable. Why? Because we do project human reality on to God and vice versa. If one assumes from the beginning that God doesn't exist, then it's reasonable to assume that we created him out of our own needs. The problem with their analyses is that they begin with the wrong assumption. God is. We confuse him with the human image not because we need to create him but because we want to suit ourselves.

16. Obviously, this is a parody of John Donne. Given its relevance as well as theological and sociological insight, the poem bears

repeating: "No man is an Island, intire of it selfe; every man is a peace of the Continent, a part of the maine; if a Clod bee washed away by the Sea, Europe is the lesse, as well as if a Promontorie were, as well as if a Mannor of thy friends or of thine owne were; any mans death diminishes me, because I am involved in Mankinde; And therefore never send to know for whom the bell tolls; It tolls for thee."

17. See Romans 8:35–39. Please take my sentence at face value and refrain from taking a theological reading on it. I realize that from the perspective of our sovereign God, some indeed may need to bear his loss. From the human perspective, however, all those who call upon the name of the Lord are included in the promise of Romans 8. Thus, anyone reading these words need never grieve the loss of God.

# Chapter 5

1. Typically, it's called the problem of sociological relativism, but it goes by other names as well (see Richard J. Bernstein, *Beyond Objectivism and Relativism* [Philadelphia, PA: University of Pennsylvania Press, 1985]). There are many elements to the problem, however, and people are differentially troubled by them. Thus, some wonder how we can have any confidence in the truth of a proposition if we know that it is sociologically relative (e.g. Karl Mannhaim, *Ideology and Utopia* [New York, NY: Harcourt, Brace and World, 1936]). Others, however, are more concerned about the theological implications, wondering how sociological relativism squares with a biblical picture of human freedom and the sovereignty of God (see Robert A. Clark and S. D. Gaede, "Knowing Together: Reflections on a Wholistic Sociology of Knowledge," *The Reality of Christian Learning*, ed. Harold Heie and David Wolfe [Grand Rapids, MI: Eerdmans, 1986]). The pastor in this story, as you shall see, is concerned with both issues, but it's the latter that is the particular problem for him.

2. This isn't an arbitrary list of characteristics, by the way. For some time now, social observers have painted a picture similar to the one found here (e.g. David Riesman, *The Lonely Crowd*; Christopher Lasch, *The Culture of Narcissism* [New York, NY: Norton, 1978]; and Robert Bellah et al., *Habits of the Heart* [Berkeley, CA: University of California, 1985]). Some of the reasons for these characteristics, along with an interpretation of their Christian significance, is provided in *Belonging* (S. D. Gaede, [Grand Rapids, MI: Zondervan, 1985]).

3. Those who use the term "secular society" do not necessarily ascribe negative characteristics to it. The classic piece in praise of secularization, of course, is *The Secular City* by Harvey Cox, (New York, NY: Macmillan, 1965). His perspective is especially interesting, I think, because he attempts to develop a Christian argument for the secular society. The best counter-argument from a Christian perspective is probably Jacque Ellul's in *The Meaning of the City* (Grand Rapids, MI: Eerdmans, 1970) and *The New Demons* (New York, NY: Seabury, 1975). Though I suspect truth lies someplace between their two positions, events since the sixties tend to make Cox's argument seem a bit naïve. Cox has offered an updated re-analysis of modern religion, by the way, entitled *Religion in the Secular City* (New York, NY: Simon and Schuster, 1984).

4. To this question, two different answers have been given. First, for those who believe that secularization is an inexorable process in modernity, new religious movements are nothing more than the last spasms of religion on its deathbed (e.g. Anthony F. C. Wallace, *Religion: An Anthropological View* [New York, NY: Random House, 1966], pp. 264–265). Second, for those who see religion as a necessary part of humanity's search for meaning, new religious movements provide continuing evidence of humanity's quest; these people hypothesize that such outbreaks of religiosity will continue to occur no matter how secular our society may become (see Rodney Stark and William Sims Bainbridge, "Secularization and Cult Formation in the Jazz Age," *Journal for the Scientific Study of Religion*, vol. 20, no. 7 [1981].

5. Obviously, the pastor's conclusion is sociologically debatable, but I think correct. This reveals my own perspective on the issue. If one assumes that human beings have an inherent need for community, security, and truth, then the existence of the modern cult is no surprise. Cults provide all of these things. Thus, even though the community they offer is totalitarian, the security they offer is illusive, and the truth they offer is heretical, modern people are attracted to them. As problematic as their content may be, their form remains highly seductive. The fact that modern cults are often populated by former Christian church members (Harold Bussell, *Unholy Devotion* [Grand Rapids, MI: Zondervan, 1984]), moreover, suggests that the church doesn't always provide an adequate response to these needs.

6. It's the value of "form over content," and thus quite dangerous, in my opinion. The pastor is to be applauded for attempting to build his church within biblical constraints. But his primary motive is the development of a certain kind of church, rather than the faith itself. The values that are dictating action, therefore, are those stemming not from the fruit of the Spirit but from the desire for a

particular kind of group experience. Thus, though the pastor is trying to be biblical, he's putting the cart before the horse. To compare this with the characteristics of the modern cult, see Ronald Enrich, *Youth, Brainwashing, and the Extremist Cults* (Grand Rapids, MI: Zondervan, 1977).

7. Anomie has many different versions, and thus definitions. It literally means "without norms" and was developed by Emile Durkheim (first in *The Division of Labor* [1893] [New York, NY: Free Press, 1964] and later in *Suicide* [1897] [New York, NY: Free Press, 1951]) to describe a condition of confusion and normative disorientation. He noted its increase in modern societies and associated it with certain kinds of suicide.

   Anomie results when something we have previously taken for granted suddenly loses its moral legitimacy. It's fleshed out especially well in Peter Berger's *The Sacred Canopy* ([New York, NY: Doubleday, 1969], pp. 81–101). One of his points, which I've made use of in the story of the pastor, is that the process of social engineering (my term) usually leads to anomie. For when we create social conditions that in turn, affect others (and ourselves), we immediately see all social conditions as a human fabrication. This is an anomic revelation because it de-legitimizes all previous interpretations that might have been assumed to exist by divine decree. What one previously thought of as "God's will" now seems to be "human invention," and the normative world appears less solid.

8. This is an offshoot of what philosophers call the *genetic fallacy*, and what theologians call *ontological dualism*. The genetic fallacy is to assume that an explanation of how something came to be believed bears on the truth value of what is believed. Thus, our pastor thought that because he understood the social conditions that brought about those "happy faces," the "happy faces" themselves must be something less than credible. He had no business assuming that, however. Dualism assumes a distinction between human events and spiritual events. Thus, once our pastor saw those "happy faces" as a human event resulting from natural sociological forces, he no longer saw them resulting from God's activity in the world. Once again, that is bad reasoning. The Bible assumes no such dualism. For a discussion of these issues in relation to sociology, please see Robert A. Clark and S. D. Gaede, "Knowing Together: Reflections on a Wholistic Sociology of Knowledge," *The Reality of Christian Learning*.

9. I'm not assuming in this example, however, that God's Spirit *was* the prime mover. The Evil One also moves in the hearts of men and women, and he's been known to be effective right in the midst of the church.

10. This is essentially the point made by Peter Berger in *Rumor of Angels* (Garden City, NY: Doubleday, 1970). What he argues is that much in our behavior and thinking reveals the assumption of some Greater Reality. For example, when a mother holds a frightened child and says "Everything's going to be all right," what does she mean? If this world is all there is, she is a liar, because she and her child are going to die; everything is not all right! If she isn't a liar, however, then her statement reveals a hope in some greater Good or Reality beyond death. Berger argues that this is also true of such things as play, humor, and damnation.

    I think Berger is correct. Humans live as if there is some cosmic significance to their lives. This doesn't prove the existence of God, by the way, since humans have been known to live deluded lives. But it does present quite a problem for the nonbeliever, in my opinion. The crucible of our beliefs, after all, is daily life. The burden of proof, existentially speaking, is on the atheist.

11. Job and Habakkuk asked such questions of God. Job's case is particularly interesting, I think, since his troubles were not his own doing. Yet, when he questioned God's wisdom in allowing him to suffer, God responded by questioning Job's right to even ask such a question. That may sound rather harsh unless we remember that, in questioning God's judgment, we set ourselves up as God's judge. When seen from that perspective, the surprising thing is that God allows us such freedom. Human beings, after all, have difficulty allowing even other human beings that freedom. God not only allows it, he has liberally sprinkled his Word with such questions. He is, in the end, an amazingly gracious and patient Creator.

# *Chapter* 6

1. Sociologists like to distinguish between two different stratification systems. One is based on acquired status, and it stratifies the population into a variety of castes. Since one becomes a member of a caste by birth, one doesn't move in or out of it readily, if at all. Thus, if one is born as an outcaste, one rarely is able to move into a more respectable caste, nor is such a move assumed to be a legitimate aspiration. (It can be done, however. See J. H. Hutton, *Caste in India* [Cambridge: Cambridge University Press, 1946], pp. 41–61, 97–100. For a general discussion of the Indian caste system see David G. Mandelbaum, *Society in*

*India*, Vol. 1 & 2 [Berkeley, CA: University of California Press, 1970]).

The other stratification system is based on achieved status, and its divisions are called classes. Here the emphasis is upon earning the accoutrements of a particular status—education, money, lifestyle, and so on. Theoretically, in such a society, it is assumed to be possible to move from one class to another, depending upon individual achievement. In practice, of course, things don't always work out that way. Many people born into a lower class, for example, find it extremely difficult to work their way up, and many in the upper classes, remain there regardless of their efforts, or lack thereof.

In the United States, we've had a mixture of caste and class. Though we've always aspired to be an open society, where people are given the opportunity to earn their status, we've periodically distributed status on the basis of racial or ethnic characteristics, an obvious example of caste (see E. Digby Baltzell, *The Protestant Establishment* [New York, NY: Random House, 1964]). For a light, non-sociological view of the American status system, the reader might enjoy Paul Fussell's *Class* (New York, NY: Random House, 1983).

2. For those interested in this contrast in organizational behavior between human beings and other animals, let me suggest chapter 4 of Peter Berger's *Invitation to Sociology* (Garden City, NY: Doubleday, 1963). His point, as you will see, is not that human behavior is any less regularized but that it is so by social influence, not innate instinct. In these chapters, too, you'll notice a distinctly deterministic orientation, even though the author isn't a determinist himself. Should you wish to see how he extricates himself from sociological determinism, you'll have to finish the book (which I recommend).

3. And, thus, the socialization of children is of paramount importance to every society. See Beatrice B. Whiting, *Six Cultures: Studies in Child Rearing* (New York, NY: John Wiley and Sons, 1963). A general review of socialization research may be found in David A. Goslin, ed., *Handbook of Socialization Theory and Research* (Chicago, IL: Rand McNally, 1969).

4. Following Sartre, I suppose one could say that it is "bad faith" to assume a responsibility was obligatory. One doesn't *have* to do anything, after all. But it would be a "bad living" to refuse all responsibilities—and in the end, not living at all.

5. In point of fact, I think the notion that ideas derive from either experience or beliefs is untenable. Quite clearly, the interaction between our thinking and doing is so complete that beliefs shape experiences and experiences shape beliefs. For that reason, the subject/object split, as used in modern science, is often mislead-

ing. I also think it doesn't do justice to the biblical picture of humanity. For a discussion of this issue in relation to the development of Western science, see R. Hooykass, *Religion and the Rise of Modern Science* (Grand Rapids, MI: Eerdmans, 1972); Michael Polanyi, *Science, Faith, and Society* (Chicago, IL: University of Chicago Press, 1959); and Richard J. Bernstein, *Beyond Objectivism and Relativism* (Philadelphia, PA: University of Pennsylvania Press, 1985).

6. Evidence of this tendency abounds, of course, not only in the media but also in the homilies of modern pastors and the literature of modern Christians. The reasons for our fascination with and all-out pursuit of self-satisfaction are complex, but a moderately good discussion can be found in Robert Bellah's, et al., *Habits of the Heart* (Berkeley, CA: University of California Press, 1985).

7. One shouldn't conclude from this that I believe environment has no influence on a child's development (I think it does) or that one shouldn't be concerned about the kind of environment in which one's child is raised (one should). But in dealing with people (children, in this case), we are dealing with a choice-making being on the one hand and an influence of unknown quality on the other. Thus, it's possible that a different child-rearing technique would have made a difference in the child's life. But that "outcome" is wholly unknown. The guilt one feels over what is essentially a "best-guess" proposition has nothing to do with biblical guilt, in my opinion. True guilt comes from disobedience to a holy God, not disobedience to some behavioral scientist's vision of human development, especially when that same vision is likely to have been generated by deterministic assumptions about the human condition (see C. Stephen Evans, *Preserving the Person* [Downers Grove, IL: InterVarsity Press, 1977]).

8. Even that possibility is debatable—not because the parent's influence is questionable, but because the parent's ability to design a positive influence is debatable. I know of few parents who are not trying to provide a good atmosphere for their children. I know of many who don't think they're succeeding very well. Why? That too is debatable. One thing is certain, however. It isn't because they aren't acquainted with modern child-rearing techniques.

9. Unless, of course, one believes that it really is the parent's accomplishment, in which case pride has little meaning, since every human accomplishment can be attributed to a prior cause. After all, the parent's ability to raise a superstar is nothing more than the result of *their* parents' child-rearing ability, which in turn is the result of *their* parents' ability, and so on. It's difficult to squeeze pride out of an infinite regress.

10. This is always where the *Beyond Freedom and Dignity* (B. F. Skinner, [New York, NY: Knopf, 1971]) debate leads. The behavioral determinists are trapped in a quagmire. To buy their argument, you have to give up any meaningful notion of responsibility. Once you do that, however, you lose not only the purpose for trying to modify behavior but also any explanation for why you would want to do it in the first place. If you give up the traditional notion of freedom, moreover, you can't even explain how it's possible to accomplish the task. It's testimony to the power of deterministic assumptions in the modern world that such illogic gets published.

11. That's why Paul can say that an officer in the church must be able to "manage his own family well and see that his children obey him with proper respect" (1 Tim. 3:4). The issue here is whether the person is capable of exercising proper authority. The home is a proving ground, says Paul. If one can't maintain order and respect within the family, then one isn't likely to do so in the local church.

   In the modern context, Paul's argument sounds deterministic. That is, it sounds as if Paul is saying, "If you're a good parent, you can jolly well make your children do whatever you want." But that isn't what he's saying. He's stating, first, that parents can and ought to control their children's behavior. That's not a matter of determinism; that's a matter of authority. Parents have the power to constrain negative behavior. If they don't employ it effectively in the family, how can they do it in the church?

   Secondly, Paul is also saying that children should be taught to respect their parents. The giving of respect, however, is a responsibility of the child, not the parent. A child in that culture was responsible to honor his or her parents. If not, the parent was to exercise discipline. Such discipline only makes sense, however, if the child is responsible for his or her actions. It assumes, one, that he or she deserves punishment (guilt), because, two, he or she chose to be disrespectful. Thus, the child is responsible for behavior and the parent is responsible to assume that fact in the way he or she disciplines.

# *Chapter* 7

1. This isn't an exaggeration. Mennonites today can be found throughout Europe and North America, as well as the USSR, Asia, South America, and elsewhere. For a discussion of Mennonite

history, see *Mennonites and their Heritage*, by Harold S. Bender and C. Henry Smith (Scottsdale, PA: Herald Press, 1964).

2. This statement could be misinterpreted. Christ was the fulfillment of messianic prophecy; thus, from his disciple's perspective, following Jesus was not anti-Jewish but the proper thing for Jews to do. Nevertheless, most Jews didn't accept Christ as their Messiah, and they viewed Jewish Christians as heretical. Jewish Christians, therefore, found themselves in the position of choosing between Christ and the Judaism of their peers. Thus, they were confronted with a choice, whether or not they wanted to be. And, of course, they chose to be free of Jewish tradition *as defined by their peers.*

3. No assumption is made here that such acts were, in fact, in accord with God's will. The issue here concerns how acts are legitimized, not whether those legitimizations were true. God may, in fact, have been displeased with some of these flights of freedom that were carried out in his name. Nevertheless, they were carried out *in his name*, not in the name of personal happiness, and therein is the crucial difference between our ancestors and ourselves.

4. The Enlightenment, of course, is a very broad movement and can't be adequately summed up by a single event, even the French Revolution. But many of the political, social, and ideological cleavages separating pre- and post-Enlightenment thought were laid bare by the French Revolution, and thus its understanding is quite illuminating. Robert Nisbet gives an astute analysis of this relationship in the first few chapters of *The Sociological Tradition* (New York, NY: Basic Books, 1966).

5. This paragraph should not have been written. It's an accommodation to efficiency and abridgment, both of which I detest. Nevertheless, it was this paragraph or nothing (a tough call) and I went with the condensed version. The reader should keep in mind, however, that this paragraph is a summary statement, subject to all the deficiencies therein. One problem with it, for example, is that the statement implies a mild economic determinism—that economic changes gave rise to social changes. In fact, I don't believe that is what happened, though surely economic and technological factors played a crucial role. Rather, I suspect that the economic changes had roots in certain social dislocations, brought on by shifts in world view (first suggested by Max Weber, *The Protestant Ethic and the Spirit of Capitalism*, trans. Parsons [New York, NY: Charles Scribner, 1958]). Others, however, see it as a primarily technological development (Jacque Ellul, *The Technological Society*, trans. Wilkenson [New York, NY: Vintage, 1964]), and the Marxists, obviously, think it can be reduced to pure economics. What this suggests is that this is a terribly

complicated subject, one that shouldn't be reduced to one paragraph.

6. The anthropological literature is especially revealing here. Often, in small communities, the severest form of punishment inflicted is expulsion from the community. This is such a powerful form of social control precisely because the individual's identity is wrapped up in the group. An Inuit, for example, doesn't think of herself as being a "member" of the Inuit community; rather she *is* an Inuit. To be expelled from the community, therefore, is to cease being the person one had been prior to the expulsion. Elenore Smith Bowen captures this quite well, I think, in her anthropologically based novel, *Return to Laughter* (Garden City, NY: Doubleday, 1964).

7. Take divorce, for example. It's a common assumption that divorce is predictable. We know that particular kinds of couples, with certain track records, are more likely to divorce than others. Social scientists tell us what factors precipitate divorce, and marriage counselors help us to avoid circumstances that might make our marriages more difficult. All of this information suggests that we understand divorce; that it's predictable.

That's just not true. Those who have studied it the most know precisely how unpredictable it is. That's why even the best marriage therapists wouldn't bet a dime on their ability to predict the future course of a marriage. They know their data is post hoc. After the divorce, they may be able to explain why it occurred. Before the divorce, however, they can provide little more than odds on its future occurrence. Theirs is a probability game, at best.

The reason has less to do with the nature of the therapists' science than the nature of their subject. Humans make choices. And, at its core, the act of independence represents the most fundamental of choices. And thus, though the choice will be tempered by circumstance and social influence, it will be a surprise. That's why divorce is unpredictable. That's also why prodigal sons sometimes come from the best of families, successful businesspeople dump the most lucrative of jobs, and theologians become the best of atheists.

8. Often we are the victims of our own independent actions. Take something as seemingly innocuous as young love, for example. I doubt there is a reader who can't remember being involved in some kind of high-school romance. That being the case, it's also quite likely that the romance ended—and not in marriage. Some such romances conclude by common agreement, but usually one person initiates the demise. Now, it's typically assumed that the one whose love is spurned is the victim in all of this. The spurned one is left high and dry, with a broken heart, and without the

former companion. Loneliness, for the spurned one, is something we would expect.

But now let me engage in true confession: I always felt just as lonely when I caused the breakup as I did when I was its so-called victim. Sometimes even more so. The reason, I think, is not that I was an abnormal teenager but that independence carried with it false promises. To justify my desire for freedom, I would overexaggerate the negative aspects of my present relationships ("she whines incessantly") and assume only the best from a replacement ("she's so mellow"). The real world, however, never succumbs to such fantasies. More often than not, my old girlfriend looked a lot better after she was gone, and my new interests—*if* they even materialized—looked a lot worse. As a result, I was left not only missing my former relationship but also living with the knowledge that my loneliness was my own fault.

Even when the termination of a relationship is wholly justified, however, loneliness can result. I've spent many hours talking with students in just such a situation. For one reason or another, they become involved with someone (friend, roommate, girlfriend/boyfriend) who is highly manipulative or emotionally exploitive. For the sake of their sanity, they dissolve the relationship, hoping to be free of harassment. When that chore is accomplished, however, they're immediately hit with self-doubt, guilt, and a relational vacuum in their lives. The guilt is often misguided, but the relational emptiness is for real. After all, the person that has been occupying much of their time and energy is suddenly absent. They miss the company. The good times. And, most of all, they miss the feeling of being needed by another human being.

9. Independence in the modern world takes many other forms, of course. Typically, when the word independence is used, people think of politics. That's not surprising, since Americans call their birthday "Independence Day" and their document of birth the "Declaration of Independence." Sometimes, too, we think of independence in relation to economic matters, as when we talk about being free from want, poverty, or even slavery. At other times, we focus on ethnic, religious, or cultural independence, as whole peoples seek to be free of discrimination or exploitation.

Though there is a certain similarity between all acts of independence, it may be helpful to distinguish between individual and collective action. A declaration of political independence, for example, is a collective act. It's accomplished on behalf of a group, and its manifest purpose is the betterment of the group as a whole. Rather than being a true act of independence, it's really an attempt to shift allegiance from one political system (e.g. King George) to another (e.g. a new republic). The assumption, of course, is that the people will be better off under the new system and possibly freer in some sense, but not that people will suddenly be independent of all governmental authority. Anarchy is rarely the purpose of a revolution.

Individual acts of independence, however, are undertaken on behalf of self, not others. They are sometimes justified as being good for another but rarely is that their intended objective. Their purpose, rather, is to free the individual from offensive social obligations. In other words, they are executed for the benefit of the actor. Period.

The distinction between individual and collective behavior is especially important when we come to the topic of forsakenness. A group seeking independence often achieves a remarkable degree of solidarity; togetherness, not rejection, is its chief characteristic. An individual in pursuit of independence, however, is attempting to break human bonds. He or she is running away from social constraints and, as such, is running headlong toward the problem of forsakenness. Individual acts of independence are not intended to produce forsakenness, of course. They purport to bring freedom and new opportunities. But intentions and outcomes are two rather different matters (see footnote #8 above).

10. See *Belonging* (Grand Rapids, MI: Zondervan, 1985) by S. D. Gaede.